AROUND Amsterdam IN 80 BEERS

Tim Skelton

Cogan&Mater

Contents

Key to symbols

🍽	Café
✖	Restaurant
🛏	Hotel
🛒	Shop
🍺	Brewery
	Tasting room
🏛	Museum
🎨	Cinema
	Theatre
🎵	Music venue
0	Place number
⊗	Closed days
🕐	Opening times
♈	Number of beers
🍴	Food
Tram	Tram
BUS	Bus
M	Metro
Train	Train

Published by Cogan & Mater Limited

© Cogan & Mater Limited 2010
Managing Editor: TIM WEBB

First Published 2010

Printed and bound in the United Kingdom by Lavenham Press, Lavenham, Suffolk.

Book design/typography: Dale Tomlinson
Typefaces: OT Versa (*by Peter Verheul*)
Maps: John Macklin

ISBN 978-0-9547789-6-5

Acknowledgements & picture credits
The publisher would like to thank all the breweries, distributors and others who have kindly given permission for their photography to be reproduced in this guide. Photos on pages 82 and 95 by Rob Gras. All other photos supplied by the author.

The original concept for the 80 Beers series came from **CHRIS POLLARD**, who also sourced many of the images for this book.

Places beers originate

▪▪▪▪	Amsterdam
▬	Netherlands
▮▮	Belgium
▬	Germany
▮▮	France
▬	USA
▭	Ethiopia

Around Amsterdam in 80 Beers has not accepted advertising or received any other form of payment or deal from any of the beer outlets featured in its pages. All entries were chosen entirely on their merits.

Welkom!

IF YOU THINK BEER needs to be yellow, shiny and familiar, this guide is probably not for you. Nor will you need us if all you want from Amsterdam is a toke and a poke.

But if you suspect that not all Dutch beer begins with an H and fancy imbibing serious liquid culture in some real temples of great pub design, read on and prepare to be pleasantly amazed.

Amsterdam may be renowned as a den of vice but it has not always been a great place for beer lovers. A few years ago it would not have been possible to produce this guide. But things have changed and very much for the better.

Stepping out of the main station and striding into the tasteless tack of Damrak – the nadir of European sophistication, with cheap pizzerias and 'Two Lips from Amsterdam' T-shirts – more delicate readers might start to wonder why they bothered to come. But make it past the tat and a vibrant city awaits, including within it a fabulous array of world class places to drink beer.

Some local brews are forgettably dull but an increasing number are well worth savouring. Some Dutch craft brewers produce beers in established Belgian styles while others are going their own experimental way. We applaud them all.

And there's no doubting that local appreciation and knowledge has improved too. Not long ago everyone here assumed 'Trappist' meant something sugary and brown that tasted even better when you added a touch of grenadine. Such days are (almost) gone. With seven cafés boasting beer menus sailing north of the 100 mark, Amsterdam can rival pretty much anywhere for choice.

If you weary of the fleshpots of the capital, 8 of our 80 entries are located 20km down the road in Haarlem – another fine city, worth at least a day trip, and great for a beery night out. Indeed it is so close to Amsterdam – 15 minutes by train – that you may consider staying there to avoid the spiralling cost of hotels in the capital.

All the pubs listed here are warm and welcoming, and many are child-friendly. Be aware though, some are also smoker-friendly, despite what the law says. Nevertheless, wherever you end up, we bet you will find something to please.

Proost!

TIM SKELTON

Listings

Places with great beer lists

- **6** Arendsnest (130)
- **8** Beer Temple (100+)
- **9** Beiaard (50)
- **17** Bruxelles (56)
- **29** Elfde Gebod (70)
- **34** Gollem (210+)
- **35** Gollem BierCafé (De Pijp) (150+)
- **36** Gollem's Proeflokaal (75+)
- **57** Old Nickel (60+)
- **69** Spuyt (100+)
- **76** Westerdok (70+)
- **77** Wildeman (218)
- **79** Zotte (130)

Breweries

- **10** Bekeerde Suster
- **44** IJ
- **63** Prael

Restaurants

- **1** 1e Klas
- **2** Admiraal
- **4** America(i)n
- **5** Amsterdam
- **18** Carillon
- **37** Gouden Reael
- **39** Haven van Texel
- **45** Jaren
- **47** Kilimanjaro
- **48** Koe
- **50** Kop van Jut
- **52** Lieve
- **65** Schiller
- **73** Vertigo
- **74** Waag

Beer shops

- **13** Bierkoning
- **20** Cracked Kettle (De Gekraakte Ketel)
- **22** Daily Deli
- **56** Mitra
- **63** Prael

Museums, concert venues & other cultural distractions

- ⑫ Beurs van Berlage
- ⑭ Boom Chicago
- ⑮ Brakke Grond
- ㉑ Crea
- ㊻ Kapitein Zeppos
- (70) Star Ferry
- (73) Vertigo

Hotels

- ④ America(i)n
- ⑱ Carillon
- (57) Old Nickel

Tasting rooms and other 'special' bars

- ② Admiraal
- ③ Aepjen
- ⑲ Chaos
- ㉓ Dokter
- ㉕ Drie Fleschjes
- ㉖ Druif
- ㊵ Heffer
- ㊶ Hegeraad
- ㊸ Hoppe
- ㊾ Koops
- (58) Olofspoort
- (60) Ooievaar
- (61) Oosterling
- (62) Pilsener Club (De Engelse Reet)
- (67) Sluyswacht
- (68) Smalle
- (72) Uiver
- (74) Waag
- (78) Wynand Fockink

Haarlem

- ⑯ Briljant
- ⑰ Bruxelles
- ⑱ Carillon
- ㊾ Koops
- (55) Melkwoud
- (64) Roemer
- (71) Studio
- (72) Uiver

The city of traders

Napoleon famously accused the British of being a nation of shopkeepers. If he was right, what does that make the Dutch?

The Netherlands has a long history as a nation of seafaring traders, which has led to the jackdaw-like accumulation and absorption of all manner of global influences and cultures. The Dutch also possess genius in marketing. Who else could convince the world that a clean but dreary corporate lager makes a fine drink and that tasteless yellow rubber is a cheese?

The city of Amsterdam owes its early prosperity to beer. And herring.

The settlement that would one day become the capital of the Netherlands eked out a living as an anonymous fishing village until 1275, when Count Floris V of Holland granted the locals exemption from paying the bridge toll everyone else was charged to cross the River Amstel. This changed everything.

The sudden right to free passage meant local traders could undercut rivals, boosting their status as travelling salesmen.

In 1323, when Willem III awarded Amsterdammers the exclusive right to import beer from Hamburg, this gave the city a virtual monopoly of the Dutch beer trade. Since the imported products were much preferred to local offerings, you can only imagine how popular this made them with local brewers.

Using the profits from the beer sales, shipping links were established that led to

an exponential growth in trade with the powerful cities of the Hanseatic League. In the 14th and 15th centuries, Amsterdam rose to become the most important city in the coastal region known as Holland.

Another major commodity was herring. Trade in that most Dutch of foods expanded after the invention of curing – gutting the fresh fish and preserving it in salt. Thus empowered, fishermen could catch as much as they wanted, sending profits skywards.

By the 16th century the first outside settlers were arriving in the city, attracted by its reputation for openness and tolerance. These included wealthy Jews fleeing Antwerp as it came under Spanish rule. Jewish influence gave Amsterdam a nickname it retains to this day, 'Mokum', deriving from the Hebrew word for place.

Amsterdammers also honed their sailing skills. Money brought by the Jews helped finance hugely lucrative voyages to

India. While other Europeans, principally the Spanish and Portuguese, were spreading the word of God in Asia and attempting to convert the locals to Catholicism, the Dutch were there to turn a profit.

Imported goods included coffee, tea and spices, and led directly to the formation of the Dutch East India Company (or VOC) in 1602. Based in Amsterdam it was the world's first multinational. It built a trading empire, primarily based around the Spice Islands – today's Indonesia.

Control of the global spice trade mattered. In the days before refrigeration spices hid many of the effects of staleness, making them as valuable as gold. With this innocent deceit came unimaginable wealth. In the 'Golden Age' of the 17th century, Amsterdam became the warehouse of the world and much of the grander aspects of the city dates from that time.

In the 18th and 19th centuries the Dutch lost much of their empire to Britain and France, though things looked up for Amsterdam when the North Sea Canal opened in 1876, giving it direct access to the sea.

The good times were back, as links with South Africa and its diamond industry made the city rich again, returning to the Netherlands an importance in the world disproportionate to its size.

Other industries thrived too. The Dutch national airline, KLM, is the world's oldest. Philips of Eindhoven is a multinational electronics giant. And then there is that brewer.

Being an international crossroads is integral to Amsterdam's soul, as evidenced by large Surinamese, Turkish and Moroccan communities and an ever-growing army of ex-pats from every which where. Around 175 nationalities are included in the city's 750,000 permanent residents.

If you want to understand Dutch business nous, visit the Heineken Experience. Ostensibly a brewery tour, in reality it is a master class in how to sell stuff. While other brewers go to great lengths to tell you why their beers are better than everyone else's at Heineken it is all about persuading you to buy bottles. And if you don't, they have still taken €15 from you for watching a two-hour long advert.

If only they put half as much effort into creating an interesting beer. For now, just be aware when the bartender presents you with a container of watery froth, topped with a head scooped to billiard table smoothness with a deft flick of a plastic spatula that they have competitions to see who is best at this.

Could anyone take beer more seriously?

The Dutch and food

...you want frietjes with that?

Dutch food is not world-renowned. Many Dutch chefs have been taught to cook well but few cook with inspiration. We suspect this is the result of attending the same catering schools that teach waiters the art of looking round attentively without seeing the person waving at them.

While this universal competence means you are unlikely to encounter the depths of mis-cooking found in many countries – did we say the UK? – you may struggle to find shining examples amid the fool's gold. While the international pub grub offered in city cafés is usually tasty, it rarely excels. We have highlighted the exceptions we know about.

As everywhere, the finest Dutch food is the simplest. Skinned and filleted lightly soused herring – Dutch sushi – eaten raw, perhaps with onion or some sweet dill pickle. Holding the beast by its tail as you lower it down your neck, this is street dining at its finest, usually confined to fish stalls and best taken by lunchtime.

One meal that has survived from Dutch colonial days is the *rijsttafel* ('rice table'), found in Indonesian restaurants. This is as Indonesian as chicken tikka masala is Indian. The concept derives from the Sumatran *nasi padang*, in which the restaurant brings you a dish of everything they have and you pay for those you eat, and pan-Indonesian *nasi campur* (or *nasi rames* – mixed rice), a one-plate meal made up of rice and a small spoonful of everything else.

Neither of those options would cut it with the hungry, businesslike Dutch, so it transformed into an institution whereby the staff bring you everything and you pay for it whether you eat it or not. Often delicious, they can contain up to twenty dishes ranging from mild to medium-spicy. *Sambal* chilli relish is on hand to pep things up.

Most *rijsttafels* for one are easily enough to feed two, though restaurants take a dim view of sharing. They prefer you to order two and waste half. Sadly, we have yet to find an Indonesian restaurant with a beer list worth mentioning.

Another national staple is chips (*frietjes*), served everywhere and invariably tasty. Increasingly these are even served with Indonesian *saté* (satay). In café-speak this usually means a giant pork or chicken kebab buried under a pint of peanut sauce with chips and/or bread on the side. A great face-filler but not terribly subtle.

Cheese fondue is an unexpected Amsterdam institution. One of the best is found at Café Bern on Nieuwmarkt (evenings only), which begs an entry here if only its beer menu were better.

Uitsmijter is a lunchtime favourite, often translated on menus as the unappetising 'two or three fried eggs

Uitsmijter

on bread'. At its worst this hit-or-miss dish means sad-looking eggs on sliced white bread, with processed cheese or ham between the two. At its best – with bacon, a decent salad garnish, and grilled melted cheese on top of the eggs – it is as satisfying as any full English/Scottish/Irish breakfast (delete by preference).

The Dutch love soups and they appear on virtually every menu. Most are average, but a winter wonder worth seeking out is *erwtensoep* – split green peas, smoked sausage, pork and carrot, with slices of rye bread (*roggebrood*) on the side. Thick and hearty, this is perfect central heating to keep out those biting winter northerlies.

The archetypal Dutch bar snack is *bitterballen*. These consist of mechanically rendered cow, ground to a mushy pulp and padded out with something grey, rolled into balls, covered in breadcrumbs and deep fried. Served straight from the fryer, their semi-liquid interior rivals the temperature of the surface of the sun, searing the lining of your mouth if you bite in too soon. Allow them to cool, then feed to the swans. Served with bland yellow mustard they sometimes reach acceptable. The one thing they are not is bitter, though we would not fault their credentials as balls.

Other popular snacks to accompany drinking (*borrelhapjes*) include blocks of cheese (*portie kaas*) and rough, peppery sausage (*portie salami*) both served with mustard. *Ossenworst*, a sausage made from minced raw steak can also be found, as can hard boiled eggs in shell, with seasoning.

For the absolute pits, watch out for the bizarre chain of hole-in-the-wall snack dispensers where inserted coins will open a little door behind which might be any manner of deep-fried object, ranging from the unhealthy to the unspeakable, including *kroketten* (large, turd-shaped *bitterballen*) and *frikandellen* (wrinkly skinless sausages). Use common sense!

Bitterballen

Beer styles – an easy guide

We have assumed that most readers have at least a basic knowledge of the beer styles found in Belgium, Germany and the UK. For those new to the game, this is a brief overview of what to expect. It is not intended as an in-depth tutorial – for better explanations please check out the *Good Beer Guide Belgium* (from www.booksaboutbeer.com).

Abbey beer
Has an abbey on the label and wants you to think it is Trappist, but cannot legally call itself such. Often a dubbel or tripel, though less strenuous styles also exist.

Altbier
German equivalent to British pale ale. Typically 4.5–5.5% alcohol by volume (ABV).

Barley wine
A beer that is strong enough to remove your ability to talk after two or three. Anything up to 12% ABV.

Blond
Usually applied to ale rather than lager, implying 6–7% ABV.

Bo(c)k
An autumn seasonal beer, similar to a dubbel in colour, strength and sometimes taste. Typically 6–7% ABV.

Bottom-fermented
A.k.a. "lager". Easier to produce in industrial quantities so less skill required. Go to Germany or the Czech Republic to taste the best of these.

Brown café (or *kroeg*)
A café that has brown walls and ceilings, traditionally from tobacco smoke, and is usually small.

Dubbel
Dark brown ale with double the malt, sometimes caramelised, typically 6–7% ABV.

Flemish old brown
Aged in oak tuns for a year or two to make a love-or-hate sour beer. Typically 5–7% ABV.

Gueuze
The supreme lambic, a sparkling drink made from blending fresh and aged lambic beers. Can shock the uninitiated, but a world classic beer style, typically 5–7% ABV.

Imperial (Russian) **stout**
Huge stouts of well-above-average strength, such as 11% ABV or higher.

Kriek
Supposed to be lambic (below) with whole cherries steeped in it (magnificent). Sometimes used to describe plain beers with cherry syrup added (tacky).

Lambic
From a family of beers made in and around Brussels, fermented like wine by yeast from the atmosphere. Unusual taste worth acquiring.

Massive ale
Dark brown, sometimes very strong and also dubbed 'quadrupel' in some quarters. Typically 9–11% ABV.

Meibo(c)k
A.k.a. lentebo(c)k. A spring seasonal, similar to a golden blond ale in colour, strength and often in taste. Typically 6–7% ABV.

Oud Bruin
Dutch style invalid's beer, usually dark and sweet. Typically 2–3% ABV.

Pale ale
Light-coloured amber ale, typically 5–6 % ABV.

Saison (Belgian)/
Bière de Garde (French)
Aged light ales, often highly hopped, sometimes magnificently. Typically 5–8% ABV.

Smoked beer (or *Rauchbier*)
Mainly lagers, made with smoked malted barley. Typically 5–6% ABV.

Stout
Dark, often chocolaty ale, darkened by the use of highly roasted malt. Typically 5–6% ABV, though some are a lot higher.

Top-fermented
A.k.a. "ale". Ferments at a higher temperature so the yeast floats. The brewer makes more decisions so skill is required.

Trappist
Produced under the supervision of monks of the Trappist Order, at one of 7 (6 Belgian, 1 Dutch) approved Trappist monastery breweries. Always worth trying, sometimes heavenly, not to a single style. Anywhere from 6 to 11% ABV.

Tripel
Strong blond ale with double the malt, typically 8–9.5% ABV.

Unfiltered
Might be left slightly cloudy to retain more flavours.

Witbier (white beer) or
Tarwebier (wheat beer)
Usually cloudy from wheat haze. Spiced when Belgian, not when German. Wheat replaces some barley in the recipe. Typically 4–5.5% ABV.

① Grand Café-Restaurant 1e Klas & 1e Klas Pub

Platform 2b, Amsterdam Central Station
T 020 625 0131
E info@restaurant1eklas.nl
www.restaurant1eklas.nl

- Daily 08.30–23.00 (No beer before 10.00)
- 9
- Dutch, pasta, steaks, quiche, rolls
- Amsterdam CS

Every great railway station must have the kind of café where intense personal dramas are played out; lovers departing for a major journey or re-united at the end of one. This dining room in Amsterdam Centraal's former first class waiting room provides such a backdrop. Tears of sorrow and joy have no doubt flowed freely here for a century and more. If leaving Amsterdam by train, you must build in a brief encounter with this place.

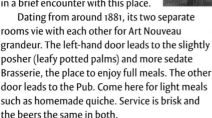

Dating from around 1881, its two separate rooms vie with each other for Art Nouveau grandeur. The left-hand door leads to the slightly posher (leafy potted palms) and more sedate Brasserie, the place to enjoy full meals. The other door leads to the Pub. Come here for light meals such as homemade quiche. Service is brisk and the beers the same in both.

Both rooms are smartly dressed, with high ceilings, large windows and wood panelling. The Brasserie is darker and bluer. The Pub has warmer tones, a central reading table and some comfy black leather armchairs at the back in case you need to flake out after a tiring day.

For such surroundings you need a *grande dame* of a beer. ▮▮ **Chimay Bleue** (9%) is just that – one of the stalwarts of the Trappist brewing tradition. Though less complex in recent years, as the brewers have cut corners to ramp up production, all things are relative. While not the classic it was, it remains a nifty, dark brown, massive ale, with enough satisfying qualities to meet the occasion.

2 Proeflokaal De Admiraal
Herengracht 319
T 020 625 4334
E info@proeflokaaldeadmiraal.nl
www.proeflokaaldeadmiraal.nl
⊗ Closed Sunday
Mo–Sa 16.00–00.00
6
Dutch
Stop/Go
1, 2, 5 (Spui)

This beautiful old building was once a stable, morphing into a distillery in 1786 and a restaurant in the 1970s. It is owned by the last of the old family distillers in the city, van Wees, who make the Ooeivaar brands of spirits. Tasting sessions can be arranged.

The décor is designed for maximum reference to its previous incarnation. Seats are ex-casks and you enter the toilets through a 10,000-litre oak tun. The centrepiece behind the bar is the water pump that used to cool the stills.

The airy glassed-in area at the front has views onto the canal, while inside is a brick-floored bar and dining room. The dungeon-like chamber visible through a grating in the floor is an old beer cellar, where they claim to put those who try to leave without paying. A spiral staircase leads to a mezzanine area. The Latin American music dilutes the authenticity.

The food has Dutch influence and includes local staples such as veal and herring.

Four of the beers come from the Friese brewery in Friesland, the northern province with its own language (Frysk) that other Dutch people don't understand. This is a cultural exchange as the brewery sells Ooeivaar spirits in return. **Us Heit Pels Speciaal** (5.5%) is a dryish, dark brown dubbel with a slightly malty taste, light enough to be a session beer.

❸ Café In 't Aepjen
Zeedijk 1
T 020 626 8401
No website
🕐 Fr–Sa 12.00–03.00; others 12.00–01.00
🍷 Beers: 14
🍴 Cheese, salami, liver sausage, apple pie
🚆 Amsterdam CS

A stone's throw from the station at the top end of Zeedijk, the 'little monkey' occupies one of the oldest wooden buildings in the city (1519 or 1546, depending on who you believe). It is also one of the oldest cafés – tiny compared to most but cavernous alongside its near neighbour, the Ooievaar (below). The one-room bar has a high wooden ceiling, copies of old masters on the walls, a curio cabinet on one side, and a simian theme throughout.

Zeedijk was once one of Amsterdam's sleaziest streets and in the 16th century this building was a hostel where sailors took 'nice young ladies'. The monkey connection came about because the one-time owner allowed sailors who had spent all their money on the women, booze and gambling to pay instead with the monkeys they had brought back from their foreign adventures.

Such a history needs a drink strong enough to slake the thirst of a sailor. ▮▮ **Kasteelbier Bruin** (11%) is a dark, unsubtle massive ale that slaps you around the face as you drink. Not so much a nightcap, more a bump on the head – a fate that can also happen on a trip to the toilet, accessed down a steep staircase missing a 'mind your head' sign at the bottom.

4 Café Americain/Eden Hotel American
Leidsekade 97
T 020 556 3010
www.edenamsterdamamericanhotel.com
Daily 07.00–23.00
6
Satay, burgers, salads, sushi, oysters, full meals,
beef Wellington, you name it.
1, 2, 5 (Leidseplein)

The grandest café in the city bar none once had a reputation for slow, surly service so bad that some wag described its waiters as 'unemployed knife-throwers'. Things have improved.

Built in 1902, this historical landmark is Art Deco grandeur in extremis, with Greco-style murals, stained-glass windows, a posse of fans whirling overhead, and brick-vaulted ceilings in a green-on-white pattern resembling a field of giant zippers. The flamboyant light fittings look like inverted parasols clustered around upended zeppelins. Drink here in splendour. How many other cafés have illuminated fountains dancing on their terrace?

The early opening is for the hotel breakfast – do not expect a beer.

Food is stylish and runs from burgers to Beef Wellington, oysters and sushi. 'Lazy Sunday' brunches feature live jazz. Part of the Eden chain, the rooms in the Hotel American above (yes, the spellings are different) are lovely but pricey. Book early out of peak times and you may find doubles at €90 – a steal for this luxury – though being close to Leidseplein it can be noisy at night.

The beer list is rubbish – we cannot pretend otherwise – but they do have the ever dependable ■■ **Duvel** (8.5%). Duvel Moortgat's distributors get the company's flagship beer into practically every bar in the Netherlands and it is often the saviour for the savvy drinker. This light-blond strong ale is the benchmark against which all others are measured. Many sore heads have borne testament to the truth of the description, 'dangerously drinkable'.

5 Amsterdam

⑤ Café Restaurant Amsterdam
Watertorenplein 6
T 020 682 2666
www.cradam.nl
Fr–Sa 11.00–02.00; others 11.00–00.00
10
Snacks, light meals (lunch), full meals International (dinner)
BUS 21, 60 (van Hallstraat/Haarlemmerweg)
 10 (van Hallstraat)

The Amsterdam began life in 1897 as a pumping station, providing extra water for a rapidly industrialising city. Old photos in the entrance hall show how it looked in its pomp. Water was pumped up the adjacent tower using four massive engines housed in the spectacular hall that became the café in 1996.

The previous owners left it in such good nick that, although some equipment had to be removed to make space, much could be left for effect. One of the massive diesel engines, itself larger than some cafés, remains intact. A chain and hook hang from a giant overhead crane on iron beams held up by iron pillars, supporting the light for the billiard table.

Floodlights have been salvaged from Ajax Amsterdam's old ground and the 1908 Olympic Stadium. The ceiling is four storeys high.

Lunch is simple pub food, with the cooking becoming more sophisticated at night. Linen tablecloths on some tables delineate the dining area. The evening menu runs from Caesar salad and oysters, through steaks, pasta and mussels, to sticky toffee pudding. The plate of *fruits de mer* comes garnished with a lobster.

In a bar named after its city, we suggest a beer brewed here too. **Natte** (6.5%) is a bittersweet, reddish-brown ale, which like the rest of 't IJ's range is brewed from organic ingredients. Sold as an Abbey-style dubbel and not a bad attempt at one.

't Arendsnest
Herengracht 90
T 020 421 2057
E info@arendsnest.nl
www.arendsnest.nl
Fr–Sa 16.00–02.00; others 16.00–00.00
130
Nuts
1, 2, 5 (Nieuwezijds Kolk)

To understand Dutch brewing, head for the 'Eagle's Nest', an elegant bar on stately Herengracht, the unofficial centre of national beer consciousness. Its list is exclusively Dutch, showcasing craft brewers and proving Benelux beers do not end at BE.

The 'Eagle' is landlord Peter van der Arend, who also runs the Beer Temple (below) and hosts tasting sessions on request (see website). He tries to fill his nest with at least one beer from each of the 50 or so Dutch breweries, although inevitably there are absentees as a few producers are too small to supply.

He also stocks 75 liqueurs and jenevers and 25 single malts. There is no food beyond nibbles, though the Lieve (below) is next door.

There are thirty beers on draught – the brass bar founts topped with a magnificent flying eagle. These include all six La Trappe beers from Koningshoeven, the Dutch Trappist brewery. Others change regularly. Well represented in bottle are smaller brewers like De Schans, Sint Servattamus, Klein Duimpje, and SNAB (the North Holland Alternative Beer Brewers Foundation).

Based in Purmerend, north of Amsterdam, SNAB started in 1991 with the aim of promoting beer culture, reintroducing old styles and promoting new ones. ▬ **Czaar Peter** (9.5%) is a Russian Imperial Stout, with bittersweet chocolate notes and a complex cocoa finish. This high alcohol style was created to survive the sea voyage from Britain to Russia. Tsar Peter I of Russia worked in Zaandam in 1697 as a carpenter.

⑦ Batavia 1920 🍷
Prins Hendrikkade 85
T 020 623 4086
E info@cafebatavia.nl
www.batavia1920.nl
🍷 Fr–Sa 11.00–03.00; others 11.00–01.00
🍺 30+
🍴 Dutch
🚆 Amsterdam CS

Designed by Dutch architect J H Slot and built around 1920, this striking building opposite the main station is a good example of the Amsterdam School of architecture, which developed in parallel with the Art Deco movement.

As old as it looks, the café only opened in 2008. Named after the former flagship of the Dutch East India Company (VOC) that was wrecked on its maiden voyage in 1629, the surviving crew members subsequently mutinying and massacring one another.

A lot of the original décor has been preserved or restored, giving a refined feel despite intrusive TV screens often showing British football for expats. Note the varnished wooden dresser where the spirits are housed. Wall plaques bear the coats of arms of various ships – this was the waterfront until an artificial island was created for the station. An overspill room is sometimes open at the back with views over the canal. At the front is a conservatory area and terrace.

Smokers are sent downstairs.

The beer list may expand but already includes noteworthy choices, such as Poperings Hommelbier and Weihenstephaner Hefeweizen. ■■ **Delirium Tremens** (9%), from the Huyghe brewery in Belgium, was voted 'Best Beer in the World' in 1997 and has never looked back. It is not the best of course – no beer is – but is still a pleasant, spiced blond ale, with a silly pink elephant logo.

8 Beer Temple
Nieuwezijds Voorburgwal 250
T 020 627 1427
E info@beertemple.nl
www.beertemple.nl
Fr 16.00–02.00; Sa 14.00–02.00;
Su 14.00–00.00; others 16.00–00.00
100+
Hamburgers, popcorn, hot dogs, snacks
1, 2, 5, 9, 13, 14, 16, 17, 24, 25 (Dam Square)

This temple to American-style craft brewing opened in September 2009 and has quickly established itself on the Amsterdam scene. Created by the owner of the Arendsnest (above) it is, for Europe, a rare specialist outlet for some of the beers that turned the US from a brewing disaster zone into one of the world's most exciting countries in which to drink beer.

Gather round the bar amid red neon lighting after dark, absorbing Americana, and join impromptu communal tasting sessions, or head for the raised mezzanine at the back for tables and more intimate drinking. There is also a small terrace out front.

Tolerate the Bud signs – they are obliged to put those up to keep the building's corporate landlords happy. There is very little crap on tap here. The beer list has already grown beyond the magic 100, with thirty taps, and more in bottle.

American beer in this sense includes a few Belgian, Dutch and Scandinavian imitators of US styles. Many are sold in 22oz

(650ml) bottles intended for sharing, including Oat Goop, an 'oat wine' co-produced by the Danish *wunderkind* Mikkeller and American brewery Three Floyds.

While you make up your mind what else to try, start with one of the permanent taps, the house brew, **Tempelbier** (6%), commissioned from Snaterende Arend, a small team of 'brewers without a brewery'. It is a blond ale with a hoppy nose and the distinctive dry-hopped bitter edge found in many an American-style IPA.

⑨ Eet & Bierencafé De Beiaard
Spui 30
T 020 622 5110
www.beiaardgroep.eu
🕐 Daily from 11.00
🍷 50
🍴 Snacks, light meals, Dutch/international
🚊 1, 2, 5 (Spui)

The original pub of a small empire of four cafés and a brewery tap sits in a prime spot close to the Singel canal, this popular spot is often full by mid-afternoon on weekends.

It has three distinct parts. From the airy conservatory you can watch trams ding their way past every few minutes. A lower, brick-walled seating area is more intimate and dimly lit, while a couple of steps higher the bar area has stools and high tables, allowing a good view of the street or down the cleavage of those in the conservatory. Above the windows are shelves crammed with beer bottles.

The lunch menu is light meals like rolls and soups. The wider evening menu always has vegetarian and fish options.

As with all the bars in this chain, go on a Tuesday and you'll get €1,00 off every bottle of 'special' beer. The others branches in town are on Marie Heinekenplein in De Pjip, just south of the centre, or at the brewery tap, Bekeerde Suster (next).

The beer range hovers around 50 with sixteen on draught. Not much to leave you wide-eyed in wonderment but enough, with Trappists well in evidence, Palm's improving Steenbrugge range and naturally some beers from their own brewery.

The people who commission ▊▊ **Corsendonk Agnus** (7.5%) will have you believe they make it themselves though it is actually brewed by Du Bocq in rural Namur. Nonetheless, the resulting medium-strength blond ale manages to be pleasant without being challenging, and is exceedingly drinkable.

10 De Bekeerde Suster
Kloveniersbrugwal 6
T 020-4230112
www.beiaardgroep.eu
Fr–Sa 12.00–02.00; Su 12.00–00.00; others 15.00–01.00
44
Rolls, wraps, hamburgers, uitsmijters, soups,
full meals (evenings only)
M Nieuwmarkt

This sprawling low-ceilinged establishment, the 'Reformed Sister', is another Beiaard outlet. In a former life it was Maximiliaans, the Netherlands' first brewpub and when Beiaard took over in 2004 they restarted the brewing tradition under a new name.

The sister in question was a prostitute who saw the error of her ways and turned to the church.

Six brews are produced at this canalside location just off Nieuwmarkt, half of them seasonal. Tours and tastings are available Wednesday and Thursday afternoons, or by arrangement.

This place is popular, but you wonder how many of the young things who come here to see and be seen actually realise it is a brewery.

In the Germanic-American brewpub tradition the shiny copper kettles are seen at the rear of the higgledy-piggledy bar. Serious steel kit is also visible through the glass doors behind.

Evening meals run to stews and steaks, with a few dishes cooked with beer, including homemade beer bread and beer butter.

The beer list includes three home-produced brews and maybe a seasonal brew. Like many brewpubs the quality can vary but the most reliable is **Manke Monnik** (7.2%), an unfiltered golden tripel with a full flavour and slightly bitter aftertaste. The 'lame monk' on its label allegedly liked a drink himself, and was crippled when an organ fell on his leg. Make of that what you will.

11 **Café Belgique**
Gravenstraat 2
T 020 625 1974
www.cafe-belgique.nl
Daily 15.00–01.00
40+
Toasted sandwiches, small snacks
 1, 2, 5, 9, 13, 14, 16, 17, 24, 25 (Dam Square)

Hiding down a side street just off Amsterdam's main shopping drag, the Belgique is one of the city's smallest and most popular cafés. Bang on the tourist trail, you won't hear many Dutch voices here. It can be standing room only with synchronized alternate breathing advisable at peak times.

Unbelievably, there is live music on Mondays.

Every inch of solid wall is covered with enamelled Belgian beer signs, apart from the curious photo of a wintery beach scene at one end. Animated conversation and loud jazz or world music are the order of the day. Low lighting is largely red, thanks in no small part to lampshades that don't let many lumens pass through.

The terrace is two benches for smokers. Food is just as limited. If you wonder what the arty doormat is all about, wait for a beer delivery and all will become clear.

A once great beer list has dwindled over the years, but still has enough distractions. Several of the eight taps are used for rotating guest beers. In bottle, ■ **Rochefort 10** (11.2%) is the supreme example of Trappist brewing. A dark, chocolate-brown seductress that demands love, though at this strength best left until later in the evening.

⑫ **Beurs van Berlage Café** 🍷
Damrak 277
T 020 530 4141
E info@beursvanberlage.nl
en.beursvanberlage.nl
🕐 Su 11.00–18.00; others 10.00–18.00
🍸 13
🍴 Breakfasts, light meals
🚂 Amsterdam CS

The Beurs van Berlage is unmissable on many levels. First, it is an unavoidable monumental structure occupying a large chunk of Damrak, just south of the station. Second, even with a passing interest in architecture, you should not miss this first and finest example of the Amsterdam School, an early 20th century modernist alternative to twiddly Art Nouveau.

Designed by Hendrik Petrus Berlage, who became the figurehead of the style and built between 1898 and 1903, it is considered the Netherlands' most important building of the period. It originally housed the stock exchange (*beurs*), although that outgrew the place within a decade. In the mid-1980s it became an exhibition hall, hosting among others the annual Bokbier festival, held in late October.

The café, with contemporary styling, occupies the original entrance hall, its magnificent brickwork interior dominated by

three tiled wall tableaux created by Jan Toorop, symbolising the past, present and future of society. The sculpted relief on the front façade, by Lambertus Zeil, shows 'Paradise', 'the Future' and 'Culture in Decay'. The leftist images did not go down well with the capitalist owners.

For something to drink that fits the mood, go for the solid and quietly dependable ■■ **Palm Speciale** (5.2%), the improving pale ale from one of Belgium's largest independent brewers, making a creditable return to form after years of semi-neglect.

13 **De Bierkoning**
Paleisstraat 125
T 020 625 2336
E info@bierkoning.nl
www.bierkoning.nl
Sa 11.00–18.00; Su 13.00–18.00;
Mo 13.00–19.00, others 11.00–19.00
1000+
None
1, 2, 5, 9, 13, 14, 16, 17, 24, 25 (Dam Square)

The 'Beer King' specialist beer shop, just off Dam Square, is in the perfect spot to catch both the passing curious and the beer geek on a mission. Unprepossessing from the outside, great things await within. It is the kind of place where you could browse endlessly, so have a plan.

They claim to stock over 1,000 different brews, and while we have neither the time nor inclination to count, it seems a reasonable estimate. The aim is to showcase the best of world brewing. Up a few steps at the back, every inch of shelving in the main showroom is crammed with brews of every taste and hue, sorted by nationality, dominated by Belgian and Dutch but with others lodged diplomatically between the local rivals.

Down below is a great selection of lambics, including oude kriek and oude gueuze. What's also refreshing is the prominence given to smaller craft brewers such as De Molen, which sometimes have trouble competing for space with the big boys.

In the counter area are hundreds of glasses, and a selection of books – including this one! Knowledgeable staff know where everything is hidden and can make helpful suggestions.

One brightly shining star is ■■ **Rulles Estivale** (5.2%), a hoppy light amber ale from the Gaume region of southern Belgium. Light in alcohol and colour, it is packed with flavour, disproving the widely held belief that good Belgian beer has to knock you out to win you over.

⑭ Boom Chicago
Leidseplein 12
T 020 423 0101 (ticket office)
www.boomchicago.nl

 Bar: Daily from 12.00. *Dinner*: Fr 19.00 (show at 21.00);
Sa 18:00 and 20:15 (shows 19.30 & 22.30);
others 18.30 (show 20.15).

🍷 20
🍴 European/Asian
🚊 1, 2, 5 (Leidseplein)

Founded in 1993, this English-language comedy theatre is an established city institution with a resident troupe of mainly American expat actors and comedians. Much of the topical stuff is about local issues so may go over the heads of visitors, but there's enough wider material to amuse. See the website for what's playing.

Shows are part scripted, part improv, with ideas seeded by the audience, guaranteeing something different every night. Tickets cost around €20 but add around €30 (excluding drinks) for a three-course meal. Mains include homemade hamburgers, tuna steaks and duck breast. Where you eat is the auditorium and drinks are brought to you even while the show is on, avoiding the need to sneak out and risk becoming a target for the rapier wits on stage.

The downstairs lobby bar is accessible to all, whether eating, laughing or neither. With few furnishings, bare floorboards, a couple of booths, and the ticket office it pumps out American rock into the evening.

Continue the American theme with a **Doggie Style Classic Pale Ale** (5.5%) from Flying Dog in Aspen, Colorado. Their 20-year quest for global domination has reached such heights that some of their brews can be found in the Netherlands' largest supermarket chain. Like many dry-hopped American pale ales, this one is either heavily hopped or over-hopped depending on your prejudice. We like it.

⑮ Vlaams Cultuurhuis De Brakke Grond
Nes 43
T 020 626 0044
www.brasseriedebrakkegrond.nl
Fr–Sa 12.00–02.00; others 12.00–01.00
22
Belgian
1, 2, 5, 9, 13, 14, 16, 17, 24, 25 (Dam Square)

On a quiet square just southeast of the Dam, the Brakke Grond is the Flemish cultural centre – a hard sell given the rivalry between the Netherlands and its southern neighbour. Flanders is promoted with style, as an unending stream of exhibitions, films, music and theatre are marshalled to convince the Dutch there is life in Europe's only other Dutch-speaking country.

The centre's café is modern and stylish, with candlelit tables and hip jazz/lounge music – think vibraphones and elevators.

Lunch (12.00–16.00) is limited to hot paninis or soup, with burgers and Flemish chips coming on line at 15.00. The excellent Belgian menu kicks in at 17.30 with delights such as mussels, cod poached in Belgian wheat beer, and Belgian chocolate mousse.

The beers are as exclusively Belgian, though the opportunity is missed to promote the smaller craft brewers. Ironically, the majority come from Wallonia, the French-speaking south. The corporate giant that appears to have a vested interest here may not know the difference.

We suggest you get thee to a monastery. ▮▮ **Chimay Rouge** (7%) is the Abbaye de Scourmont's contribution to the portfolio of dubbel-style beers. Reddish brown in colour, it is less sweet and more bitter than most of its rivals.

16 Café Briljant

Lange Annastraat 33, Haarlem

T 023 542 2925

E info@cafebriljant.nl

www.cafebriljant.nl

⊗ Closed Monday & Tuesday

🕐 We–Th 17.00-01.00, Fr 17.00–03.00;
Sa 16.00–03.00; Su 16.00–01.00

🍷 40+

🍴 Nibbles

🚆 Haarlem, then Bus 300 (Centrum/Verwulft)

This friendly, quietly Bohemian suburban beer bar is down a residential street just south of central Haarlem, and very much worth seeking out. To find it head west from the bus stop at bustling Botermarkt, down Tuchthuisstraat, then shimmy left and right into Lange Annastraat. The snug, wooden-floored café is on the left.

Live music events (from 21.30) on most Thursdays and some Sundays may include the upright piano in the bar. The first Thursday of each month is Open Mike Night, where pretty much anything goes if you fancy yourself as a troubadour. At other times unobtrusive R&B and the likes of Joan Baez and Johnny Cash rule the sound system.

If you do need a change from beer, there is a fine range of single malts.

The beer list may expand courtesy of its beer-loving owner. The current crop is mainly Dutch and Belgian, including seven Trappists, most stuff from local Jopen, St Bernardus and de Ranke's XX Bitter. Erik de Noorman, a barley wine by Klein Duimpje from south of Haarlem is there too, as is their house beer, ▬ **Briljant Bier** (7.2%), a refreshing light dry-hopped golden tripel with just a hint of coriander.

⑰ Café Bruxelles 🍷 ✕

Lange Wijngaardstraat 16, Haarlem

T 023 531 4509

www.cafebruxelles.nl

🕐 Th–Sa 17.00–02.00; others 17.00–01.00

🍷 56

🍴 International

🚆 Haarlem

To find this popular café-cum-eatery from Haarlem station, take the main route to the Grote Markt, till you reach Smedestraat on your left. It is in a side street off that.

While the outside is an unassuming shop front, inside is arty and stylish in a studenty kind of way. The fantasy wall paintings are half Roger Dean, half Ninja Turtle. We can agree colourful. Downstairs this is offset by a lovely oak-beamed wooden ceiling. Upstairs in the dining room it is not, making it seem even brighter.

If coming to eat, try to book ahead as the tables fill up, especially at weekends, though you can often eat at the bar without a reservation, even when it is quite busy. The food includes a good value daily special, the '5½ euro *hap*' (snack) – often a bowl of pasta. Other mains include the two xylophone classics, spare ribs and rack of lamb.

The beer list is the best in Haarlem. Most are Belgian, with a few Dutch thrown in. Check out the chalkboard for the five beers of the month on the changing guest taps. ▮▮ **Poperings Hommelbier** (7.5%) is a superb pale amber ale from West Flanders with finely balanced, peppery hopping. Its lightness of touch conceals its alcoholic strength, rendering it quaffable or dangerous, depending on your viewpoint.

18 Hotel Carillon ⊕ ⊗ ⊜
Grote Markt 27, Haarlem
T 023 531 0591
E info@hotelcarillon.com
www.hotelcarillon.com
⊙ Daily 12.00–23.00
🍷 13
🍴 Soups, rolls (lunch); modern Asian (dinner)
🚂 Haarlem

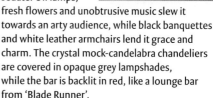

The friendly Carillon, on Haarlem's main square, ten minutes' walk from the station is quiet and sedate. Oil lamps, fresh flowers and unobtrusive music slew it towards an arty audience, while black banquettes and white leather armchairs lend it grace and charm. The crystal mock-candelabra chandeliers are covered in opaque grey lampshades, while the bar is backlit in red, like a lounge bar from 'Blade Runner'.

For old school reality, the terrace is metres from the imposing St Bavo's Cathedral.

Upstairs is a budget hotel with clean en suite doubles and all-in breakfast. No lift, steep staircases to the third floor and the corridors smell a bit stale but many rooms look straight out at the cathedral. The cathedral bells are loud but atmospheric; the booming music from the neighbouring Café Studio (below) into the early hours, is not.

The restaurant opens from 07.30 for coffee and apple pie, but you won't get a beer before noon. Light lunch carries on till 17.00, before an evening menu of Asian fusion cuisine, including teriyaki, kicks in until 22.00.

▬ **Jopen Stout** (5.5%), from Haarlem's sort-of-local brewery is a dark black beer that punches well above its weight. In the bottle it is an accomplished and nicely balanced blend of rich chocolate and coffee flavours with a slightly bitter finish.

19   **Café Chaos** 🍷

Looiersgracht 144

T 020 623 5269

🕐 Daily 12.00–01.00

🍸 10

🍴 Toasted sandwiches, uitsmijters, soups, snacks, salads, tapas

🚌 142, 170, 172 (Raamplein), Stop/Go (Looiersgracht)

🚊 1, 2, 5 (Leidseplein), 7, 10 (Raamplein)

At last, a curiously named cafe that does what it says on the sign.

Do not be surprised by the thick carpet of discarded peanut shells that start as soon as you walk through the door. When crushed they release a small amount of oil that is good for the

wooden floor. There is no sneaking around here. Your very presence may also provoke comment. This is the kind of friendly local bar where a new face sparks discussion. But don't be put off – friendly means friendly.

A large, darkened, mock-Rembrandt oil painting adorns one wall. A cloud of cherubs hangs from the ceiling, filling every available space above head height, staring down at you, interested in your every move. Bob Dylan or Abba or 'Yes Sir I Can Boogie' provide the soundtrack.

In summer tables and chairs perch on a precarious sloping canalside terrace with no barrier – don't sit with your back to the water if you've had a few…

Written on one wooden ceiling beam in Dutch are words that translate roughly as, 'Not everyone understands beer, but those that do drink it here'. We are not aware of this becoming a new Duvel Moortgat catchphrase but they supply the highlights here, including Maredsous and La Chouffe.

Rarer-to-find in Amsterdam is the darker ■■ **McChouffe** (8.5%), a dark brown Scotch ale with faint hints of liquorice. Since the tiny Achouffe brewery was absorbed into the Duvel empire it has enjoyed far greater distribution but continues to be made at its original home in southern Belgium.

Cracked Kettle (Gekraakte Ketel) 20

 Cracked Kettle Amsterdam
Raamsteeg 3
T 020 624 0745
www.crackedkettle.com
⊙ Daily 12.00–22.00
🍷 500+
🍴 None
🚊 1, 2, 5 (Spui)

This beer shop is one of those heart-warming places where every inch of space is devoted to helping customers discover new and exciting things. The ethos is to concentrate on small independents and to steer clear of bland corporate brands.

Via its website you can order over 1100 brews from an online store, with shipping possible worldwide. Only about half of those will physically fit in the shop. The lower area contains mainly Dutch and Belgians. On the slightly cramped upper floor there are offerings from round the world.

Sadly the beers cannot be sampled on the premises but with the Gollem beer café (below) literally just across the street, you are unlikely to die of thirst.

One beer seldom found in local cafés is ▮▮ **3 Fonteinen Oude Geuze** (6%), a beautifully balanced example of an *oude gueuze*, with a little less tartness than some. If you do not know authentic gueuze, do not approach it as a beer. Fermented using airborne, or 'wild' yeast, it is a little like beer that has been fermented in the way of a vintage wine.

For better or for worse, it is the author's favourite lambic. To understand more we suggest you buy a copy of our sister publication, LambicLand. But then we would, wouldn't we.

21 CREA Café 🍷 ✕ 🌀
Turfdraagsterpad 17
T 020 525 1423
E info@creacafe.nl
www.creacafe.nl
🕐 Su 11.00–19.00; others 10.00–01.00
🍸 13
🍴 Breakfast, toasted sandwiches, rolls, snacks, soups
🚋 4, 9, 14, 16, 24, 25 (Spui/Rokin)

CREA is the cultural organisation of the University of Amsterdam. Officially a student bar, the café attracts a broader clientele thanks to its quiet location on the south side of Grimburgwal, one of the city's tiniest canals. From the north, you will get within a few metres of its white-painted front before a frustrating 100-metre detour via the nearest bridge. Pole vaulting is discouraged.

The café sprawls over several rooms in bright monochrome shades (turquoise, red ochre, then orange). Less wearing are the potted palms and Middle-Eastern lanterns, adding an eclectic feel to the swan-strewn stretch of water beyond the panoramic windows at the front. They manage to squeeze in a small waterside terrace.

Entertainment is provided by locals feeding these birds, while flocks of rowdy gulls peck frantically at their heads to steal their booty. That's the swans' heads, not the locals' – this isn't Hitchcock.

Music (mainly blues) is loud but not deafening. If you prefer it live, there is an open podium night on the second Thursday of the month (Sep–Jun). Limited food options include a yoghurt and muesli breakfast.

In another nod to its student core, there is no table service, only bar sales as in a British pub. The best beers are from Duvel Moortgat, including both Maredsous 10 and its little sister, ▐▌ **Maredsous 8** (8%). This excellent dark brown ale, brewed by agreement with the Abbaye de Maredsous in Belgian Namur, is deceptively strong for a dubbel.

Daily Delis

Christiaan Huygensplein 36

T 020 468 7711

E info@dailydelis.nl

www.dailydelis.nl

⊗ Closed Sunday & Monday

Tu–Fr 11.00–19.00; Sa 10.00–17.00

75

Italian, tapas and more

 9 (Kruislaan)

Easily accessed via tram 9, if some way from the centre, this friendly deli cum corner shop on a modern residential square in southeast Amsterdam is worth finding for the rare beers it stocks.

Pride of place food-wise goes to the homemade tapenades, grilled vegetables, Spanish tortilla, organic quiches and soups in the chilled display cabinet at the back. There are herbs and spices, coffees, teas, organic produce, Italian delicacies and ceramics too.

The beer range is quality rather than width, featuring local brewers De Prael and 't IJ, some hard-to-find Belgians like Dupont and St Bernardus, German Weihenstephaner's full range, American contributions from Saranac, and even unusual British ales like Old Slug Porter from RCH in Weston-super-Mare.

The Netherlands' one world-class extreme microbrewery is in the town of Bodegraven, 30km south of Amsterdam. Living the Dutch dream, Brouwerij de Molen (Mill Brewery) operates out of a 1697 windmill, De Arkduif, after Noah's dove. Their beers are sold in wax-sealed, individually numbered bottles, the labels showing brewing and bottling dates, and the number of bottles in each batch.

The outstanding **Hel & Verdoemenis** (10.2%), or 'Hell & Damnation' is an Imperial Stout that pours with a head the colour of milky coffee. There are hints of bitter coffee in a smooth, almost smoky aftertaste – like alcoholic dark chocolate with a hazelnut in the middle. The label says this will keep for 25 years, but you may be too impatient to test whether this is true.

⑳ Café De Dokter ♟
Rozenboomsteeg 4
T 020 624 2582 (daytime); 020 626 4427 (evenings)
E info@cafededokter.nl
www.cafe-de-dokter.nl
⊗ Closed Sunday & Monday
🕐 Tu–Sa 16.00–01.00
🍷 10+
🍽 Cheese, smoked sausage
🚋 1, 2, 5 (Spui)

Claiming to be Amsterdam's smallest bar, the 'Doctor' was founded by a surgeon from a nearby former hospital, and was initially the hangout of doctors and medical students. The couple who have run it for the last four decades are the sixth generation of the family who were originally handed the keys back in 1798.

The interior is archetypal brown café. The walls and ceiling are never cleaned. Cobwebs hang from the light fittings and brass instruments, which clutter in one corner. There is a birdcage that is so dust-encrusted that you wonder if its last occupant suffocated. The serving surfaces on the other hand are pristine.

This great little pub is a must-visit stop on any tour of the city. Louis Armstrong and Billie Holliday fill the air of its single tiny room, barely lit by candlelight. Reaching the toilet upstairs requires acrobatic skills on the precipitous spiral staircase.

Food is limited to cubes of cheese or smoked sausage, though if you are hungry you could try the owners' bistro (Beems), round the corner at Rokin 74.

The lack of space means there is nowhere to stock a large range of beer, though they manage ▬ **König Ludwig Weissbier** (5.5%) from Bavaria. Refermentation in the bottle produces a sparkling and refreshingly fruity brew, which the brewery claims is the oldest wheat beer in Bavaria, linking it back to the Bavarian royal family, with exclusive brewing rights for over two hundred years. The Bavarians might usefully teach the rest of Europe how a great wheat beer can taste.

24 Dopey's Elixer
2e van der Helststraat 52a
T 020 671 6946
www.datandzone.nl/dopeyselixer/joomla
Fr 12.00–02.00; Sa 16.00–02.00; Su 16.00–01.00;
others 12.00-01.00
28
Soups, snacks, daily specials
12, 25 (Cornelis Troostplein)

Despite the daft name (we don't get it either), Dopey's has been in business since the Sixties and is one of the longest-standing brown cafés in increasingly fashionable De Pijp. By day the locals in this quiet residential area might sit at the bar reading the paper, listening to Dutch talk radio or just chatting with the landlord. Outside a few wooden benches are for people watching, or smoking.

Inside, one end of the dark bar opens into a kind of conservatory, where for little amusement, you can grab a window table and watch the near misses on the crossroads outside – one of those confusing Dutch junctions with priority to the right, where if several cars turn up at once nobody knows who has right of way.

Six days out of seven, food is hearty but limited. Wednesday evening is 'gastronomic night', with a popular and ever-changing three-course dinner. Book ahead.

The draught beers are mainly dull global brands but there is some good stuff among

the bottled list, including several lambics from Boon and a healthy scattering of Trappists.

■■ **St Bernardus Prior** (8%) hails from the St Bernard brewery in Watou, close to Belgium's border with northern France. Originally set up to brew on a commercial scale for the abbey of St Sixtus at Westvleteren, they have long since set their own course with highly credible results. This sweetish, strong dark dubbel has the same hints of pear drop in the nose as the brewery's other strong beers.

㉕ **De Drie Flesches**
Gravenstraat 18
T 020 624 8443
Su 15.00–20.00; others 12.00–20.30
2
Snacks only
1, 2, 5, 13, 17 (Dam Square)

The 'Three Bottles' is a fabulous old spirits tasting room next to a hotel of the same name in the heart of the city. It has been serving alcohol since 1650 and has been part of the Bols empire for almost half of that time.

There are actually more like a hundred bottles here. Corporate run it may be, but it is still unmissable for its olde worlde charm.

The wooden-floored bar was lit by ancient gaslight fixtures until recently. Lining one wall are rows of barrels, with nothing between them and the bar except customers. The smaller barrels are privately owned, filled with the drink of the owner's choice, and accessible only via a private key to the tap. Lending a client the key for a crafty snifter is a great way to soften them up.

The larger casks are just for show. There is one table, otherwise it's standing room only. The sole soundtrack is the relentlessly soporific ticking of the clock on the back wall, which chimes every quarter hour to check you have not nodded off.

This is not a beer bar – you can count the choices on your thumbs – but they do have guest beers such as ■■ **Maredsous 10** (10%) from Duvel Moortgat. This strong ale is billed as a 'tripel', though it is closer to a blond barley wine. It is warming, but the high alcohol content can be missed. Be warned.

26 Café De Druif
Rapenburgerplein 83
T 020 624 4530
⊗ Closed Tuesday
🕒 We–Mo from 15.00
🍷 8
🍴 None
🚊 9, 14 (Mr Visserplein)
🚌 22, 42, 43 (Kadijksplein)

Many cafés in Amsterdam claim to be the oldest. The 'Grape' makes the more modest assertion of being 'third oldest'. Whether this statement is any more or less true than the other is a matter for discussion though it certainly *sounds* believable. The interior is as glorious as it is authentic, though despite this, it remains more of a locals' hangout.

Some say Dutch sailor and folk hero Piet Heyn was a customer here, which is less likely, as it opened in 1631, two years after his death.

It is a split-level affair – down below, the bar area has a table, a park bench and a few stools, with jenever barrels behind the bar. There are more tables on the upper level, five steps higher.

The only nod to the name are the plastic grapes hanging from the lamps. The real theme is fishier, with pictures of herring and photos and models of herring boats.

❚❚ **Westmalle Trappist Dubbel** (7%) is arguably the safest and least challenging of the Trappist ales and the most widely available in the Netherlands. Are these facts related? Draw your own conclusions. Safe does not mean dull in this case. The appeal of this dark brown, chocolaty dubbel will become clear when you try it.

De Dwaze Zaken 👤 ✗

Prins Hendrikkade 50

T 020 612 4175

E eten@dwazezaken.nl

www.dwazezaken.nl

🕐 Th–Sa 12.00–01.00; others 12.00–00.00

🍷 21

🍴 Snack, soups, rolls and hearty mains

🚆 Amsterdam CS

Another first for the 80 Beers series. The 'Funny Business', opposite Centraal Station, is a "Christian arty café" adjoining a Christian bookshop.

Apart from a wall mosaic behind the bar, showing a woodland scene in pastel shades with a Sacred Heart cross and red-tiled walls to the side bearing proselytising messages, the religious aspect is low key. It is more of a fashionable eatery, with wooden floors and palm fronds to the fore.

By day background jazz and crooning fails to interrupt the animated conversations of young couples and hot debate of middle-aged housewives occupying most of the tables, though after dark the industrial-strength speakers take over. There is live Jazz on Thursdays.

Food is wholesome and genuinely homemade. Hearty soups come with hunks of bread and if healthy mode has descended, there is a range of fresh fruit juices.

The beer list includes numerous beers with abbey connections of course – Maredsous, Karmeliet, Chimay and others. Respectful of this theme we suggest ▊▊ **St Bernardus Abt 12** (10%), a dark, strong and satisfying beer that comes with a pear drop aroma. More than one would definitely bring out your spiritual side.

Before leaving we recommend readers to pass water here. The mosaic-tiled inner chambers are works of art of the wonky Gaudi school – a loo with a view.

28 Café Eik en Linde
Plantage Middenlaan 22
T 020 622 5716
www.eikenlinde.nl
Fr–Sa 11.00–02.00; others 11.00–01.00
20
Soups, rolls, snacks, toasted sandwiches
9 & 14 (Plantage Kerklaan)

The original 'Oak and Lime' tavern, in early 19th century Amsterdam, had a dodgy reputation. In 1863 that building was absorbed into the expanding Artis Zoo complex, where it became the wolf house. A plaque still commemorates its former life.

The current café, on a busy street a few hundred metres up the way, is its fourth incarnation and dates from 1967. It is the sort of one-room brown café people pop into or sit outside for a swift one while walking the dog. Its walls are covered with paintings, old photographs and memorabilia. You may be the only customer who lives more than a few blocks away, so prepare to chat.

The bar stools clustered around the counter bear testament to the fact that chatting is the main entertainment – along with billiards. The periodic whining sound is the timer for the lights, warning players to feed in another coin before darkness descends. Windows at the back look out onto a small garden.

The beer list contains few surprises, though there is Orval among several Trappists (rare for a brown café) and 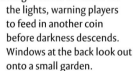 **Paulaner Hefeweizen** (5.5%) is here on draught. This is another example of a Munich brewer showing the rest of the world how to do a golden-amber wheat beer properly. It is unfiltered with a wheat haze, its flavour nicely balanced, with fruit and spice notes and a hint of bitterness.

㉙ Het Elfde Gebod
Zeedijk 5
T 06 3062 6373 (mobile)
⊗ Closed Sunday to Tuesday
🍷 We–Sa 17.00–01.00
🍸 70
🍴 Snacks
🚂 Amsterdam CS

The 'Eleventh Commandment' is *voluptatibus fruendum* ("Thou shalt enjoy life").

Another of the clutch of fine bars at the top end of Zeedijk, from the street it can appear crowded and cramped. Most customers hover round the counter at the front, blocking the view of free tables at the back. The front is bare-floored, the rear carpeted. Watch the small step down between the two.

Behind the bar, bottles (including a good range of jenevers) are housed in glass-fronted cabinets. The wood panelling on the walls stops short of the ceiling allowing room for (mostly religious) bric-a-brac on a shelf above. The ecclesiastical theme continues with the pews down one side – designed more for awkward penitent perching than comfortable reclining.

The music is background late-night soporific, even early in the evening. Think Billie Holiday and Tom Waits. Food is survival rations only, so with a beer list this good you may want to line your stomach beforehand.

The list is exclusively Belgian, with standouts including Poperings Hommebier on tap, three from St Bernard, and several from Dupont and Achel. De Ranke's wonderful ▌▌ **XX Bitter** (6.2%) is in our view one of the best beers made anywhere – simple as that. It is a terrific, dry, blond-amber ale that manages to stay well-balanced while packing an impressive hoppy bitter punch.

Elsa's Café
Middenweg 73
T 020 668 5010
www.elsascafe.nl
 Fr–Sa 11.00–02.00; Su 13.00–01.00, others 11.00–01.00
 35
Dutch pub grub
9 (Hogeweg)

On trusty tram route 9, with a stop right outside, this brown café in southeast Amsterdam, a few doors from the Mitra off-licence (below), began life as a tram waiting room in the 1890s, and evolved from there.

Billing itself as a home from home, it is inspired by and named after Elsa Maxwell, the American gossip columnist and socialite famed for organising parties for New York's elite between the wars. Hence the bar's motto: 'The Hostess With the Mostest'.

Sit on the terrace tram spotting or enjoying the view of the park across the road. Inside, large windows give an airy feel by day while Art Nouveau lighting and wall paintings evoke *fin de siècle* elegance – more so when Mariah Carey is not droning away over the speakers.

The food is advertised on large blackboards, with the usual soups, rolls and steaks, with a few snails crawling around somewhere in between.

The beer selection is shrinking but still not bad. There is welcome coverage of Amsterdam brews, from both 't IJ and De Prael. The latter's **Mary** (9.7%) is a hefty, bittersweet amber tripel with a slight fruity aftertaste. Like all De Prael's beers, it is named after iconic Dutch singers of old – in this case Mary Servaes, who worked under the stage name of 'Zangeres Zonder Naam' – the Unnamed Singer. Ironic, eh?

Café De Engelbewaarder
Kloveniersburgwal 59
T 020 625 3772
Fr–Sa 11.00–03.00; Su 14.00–01.00; others 11.00–01.00
18
Toasted sandwiches, pasta (lunch);
Dutch and European main meals (dinner)
M Nieuwmarkt

The 'Guardian Angel' began life in the 1970s as a literary café with, in those days, the best range of ales in Amsterdam. The emphasis has since shifted from words to music – mainly jazz – with a side order of food. The beers now come from the large Belgian independent, Palm.

In an old townhouse, two minutes' walk from Nieuwmarkt, it has a welcoming vibe, despite an unprepossessing, narrow entrance up steep stone steps. Tables at the front look out over the canal, with a more expansive seating area at the back. A stove provides warmth on wintery days and a canalside terrace cools in the summer. Catch the Sunday afternoon jam session from 16.30.

Lunches are basic, while dinners (from 17.30) can include hearty home cooking such as sausage with *boerenkool* (curly kale), a traditional dish rarely seen on café menus.

The eleven draught beers include Palm's unfiltered Speciale, a Rodenbach and several Boon lambics. There are 75cl bottles too but

the refreshingly sharp, citrussy ▌▌**Boon Oude Lambiek** (6%) on tap, is a rare find anywhere.

Palm own 50% of Frank Boon's brewery, which sits on the banks of the Senne, south of Brussels. Boon is a master lambic maker, his beers fermented using only yeast from the atmosphere – so expect cidery and vinous character rather than beery. 'Oude' (old) in this context means aged in a huge oak barrel for over two years and served up unblended and undiluted. Each cask is subtly different but never dull.

Café Genootschap der Geneugten
Kerkstraat 54
T 020 625 0934
Fr–Sa 20.00–03.00, others 20.00–01.00
45
None
1, 2, 5 (Keizersgracht or Prinsengracht)

The 'Pleasure Club' (no, not that) sets out its stall early with loud Tamla Motown, slewing Hendrix-wards later. On our last visit it was young Bohemians and bearded John Belushi lookalikes.

Close to noisy Leidseplein, sophisticated Art Deco is trimmed with earthy elements like loud rock and fruit machines, more commonly found in the pack-'em-in, tank-'em-up establishments around the corner. In the middle is a fascinating little brown café with wooden floorboards and wood-panelled walls, just about shining through.

It cannot decide whether to be a cocktail bar or a beer pub. French film posters and brewery adverts adorn the walls. The jester's head and pink elephant behind the counter suggest a place that does not take itself too seriously. Peaceful cohabitation is achieved, without either old or young alienating the other.

There's enough of interest on the beer list to make it worth a detour, plus there are around 40 jenevers and other locally produced spirits. Dupont's Moinette Blond is sold in 33 and 75cl bottles. Other Belgian independents include Slaghmuylder and Halve Maan.

Best of the bunch is De Ranke brewery's █▌**Guldenberg** (8.5%), brewed in the small Belgian town of Dottignies, not far from Lille. This dry-hopped, blond tripel has a lovely bitterness that's just about kept in check by the addition of a little candy sugar.

33 Gent aan de Schinkel 🍷 ✕

Theophile de Bockstraat 1

T 020 388 2851

E gentaandeschinkel@planet.nl

www.gentaandeschinkel.nl

🕐 Fr–Sa 11.00–02.00, others 11.00–01.00

🍷 26

🍴 Light lunches, full dinners

🚊 1, 17 (Surinameplein)

🚌 15 (Haarlemmermeerstraat)

This convivial corner café is in a quiet neighbourhood beyond the southwest end of Vondelpark. On foot, leave the park by its western exit, go straight on for a hundred metres, cross the canal and you are there. It is three blocks south of the tram stop, or a couple of minutes' walk from the bus.

The bar has a wooden floor, well-worn tables, and a line of upholstered stools rubbed threadbare by a steady stream of backsides, bearing testament to this place's appeal. Red velvet curtains add a touch of warmth, while the light fitting above the bar looks like a disembowelled video cassette thrown in the air and cast in metal. (It's art.)

Although you cannot see the adjacent Schinkel canal from the cosy wooden-decked terrace, it is one of Amsterdam's busiest waterways and you may be treated to the surreal experience of the nearby swing bridge opening, letting a 30-metre cargo barge glide past at eye level, barely beyond arm's reach.

Lunch is limited but dinner is more varied, including fish and meat dishes dispensed from the open kitchen at the back.

The beer list includes eight Trappists plus various other Belgians including ▮▮**Straffe Hendrik** (9%), from Bruges. This dry, golden amber beer returned to its home city and the revamped Halve Maan brewery in 2008, at which point it was upgraded to a tripel. This enhanced its flavour and it remains highly drinkable.

34 Café Gollem
Raamsteeg 3
No phone
E info@cafegollem.nl
www.cafegollem.nl
Fr–Su 14.00–02.00; others 16.00–01.00
210+
Bar snacks (olives, cheese, salami)
 1, 2, 5 (Spui)

When it opened in 1974, Gollem was Amsterdam's first proper specialist beer café, and alongside the Wildeman still boasts the widest selection in the city.

The appeal of this institution is obvious as soon as you walk through the door. The cramped bar area helps get it rated as the capital's favourite drinking hole – at peak times it can resemble the stateroom scene from the Marx Brothers' *A Night at the Opera*. A sitting area up a few steps on a mezzanine at the back offers some respite and marginally more breathing space.

The walls are lined with old beer bottles, suitably brown. Ladies need to brave the mouldy, cold and cobwebbed loos, while gentlemen face a height problem. The tall must mind their head and the vertically challenged may need tiptoe to reach the curiously elevated bowl. Thankfully more attention is paid to input than output, as it should be.

The 12 taps and 200 or so bottled options, listed on blackboards on the walls, include most Trappists, Van Eecke's Kapittel range, almost everything from the Dolle Brouwers, numerous Boons, Slaapmutske and regularly changing guests.

A world-class beer café demands a beer equal to it – **Saison Dupont** (6.5%), the golden blond, herbal and hoppy blonde ale from the Dupont brewery – fits the bill perfectly. Its slightly weaker organic twin – the Biologique – is also available if you want to want to explore the merits of green brewing.

The Cracked Kettle beer shop (above) is directly opposite.

Biercafé Gollem
Daniel Stalpertstraat 74
T 020 676 7117
E info@cafegollem.nl
www.cafegollem.nl

Fr–Su 14.00–02.00; others 16.00–01.00

150+

Snacks, tapas and dim sum

16, 24 (Ferdinand Bolsstraat)

Gollem has spawned a second café, in the increasingly trendy De Pijp district, south of the canal ring. This popular gathering spot is another of the city's best beer cafés and a must-do for anyone wanting to drink serious beer in lovely surrounds. Slightly off the beaten track there are more regulars than tourists here.

It is cavernous compared to the original, though similar in concept – a bar area at the front with raised seating at the back. It is big enough to have a few tables – not many, mind. From the tram stop head away from the city centre and it is the second street on the left.

Best enjoyed in the afternoons, when laid-back jazz and R&B fills the air. It rarely becomes loud enough to interfere with talk of tasting notes with beer-loving strangers at the next table. It gets rowdier in the evenings, especially at weekends.

With in excess of 150 beers to choose from, you are bound to encounter old friends in a range not dissimilar to the mothership. Well represented among the regulars are the

Dolle Brouwers, 'the Crazy Brewers', from West Flanders. Among their creations is **Oerbier** (9%), a strong, dark brown ale with the hearty satisfaction of a powerful Trappist, but sour notes that hint at oak ageing.

36 Gollem's Proeflokaal

Overtoom 160–162

T 020 612 9444

E info@cafegollem.nl

www.cafegollem.nl

Fr–Su 14.00–02.00; others 16.00–01.00

75+

Snacks and beer specials

1 (1e Constantijn Huygensstraat); 3, 12 (Overtoom)

A proeflokaal is a tasting room. This one was already well-established as a place to try beers, wines and spirits before its recent incorporation into the growing Gollem empire. Since the move it has veered towards beery, though a decent selection of wines and single malts has been retained.

Unlike the other Gollems, there is real food here, with daily specials adopting a a theme of cooking with beer, such as chicken in a beer sauce or rabbit cooked in kriek.

22 taps line the bar, begging you to sit down and get comfortable. Empty bottles line the walls, with wall space taken up by enamel brewery signs. The chalkboard menu does not quite scale the heights of its sister cafés, but the selection is well chosen – you would be more than happy to take most home to meet the parents.

If you don't know what to order, duck the Pils but otherwise close your eyes and point. As well as most Trappists you will find Corsendonks, Deliriums, Brugse Zots, Witkaps, and several from 't IJ.

One less frequently seen Trappist is ▮▮ **Achel Blond** (8%), a well-balanced, almost-too-drinkable tripel from the 'new' Trappist brewery founded in 1999 at the Achel cloister. Bang on the Belgian border, south of Eindhoven, a painted line runs across the compound defining the two countries. The building has two postal addresses but the brewing kit is definitely on the Belgian side.

③ De Gouden Reael
Zandhoek 14
T 020 623 3883
www.goudenreael.nl
Daily from 16.00 (dinner from 18.00)
12
French
 3 (Planciusstraat), or Bus 48 (Silodam)

A Golden Real was an old Spanish coin. The café that takes its name occupies a picturesque waterside spot in a gentrified dockland location that is now one of the prettiest neighbourhoods in the city, about 1.5 km west of Centraal Station.

Built in 1648, the stepped gable building was originally a warehouse for storing herring. Back then Zandhoek was the waterfront where fish was unloaded. It sits beside an old white-painted wooden drawbridge, best seen from its terrace. The Reael family were politicians in the city during the Golden Age and placed the 'golden coin' in the front gable.

In the mid 19th century it became a bar for local labourers, immortalised in a 1940 novel by Jan Mens, set in and named after it.

Despite the history, it does not feel dated. The front bar area is dominated by impressionist paintings – French music fills the air. At the back, there are candlelit tables on a mezzanine dining area above the kitchen. Mouth-watering smells

waft everywhere, from a long list of French bistro classics with a nod towards Alsace-Lorraine, with quiche and *choucroute*. You will also find pâté, 'steak frites' and *sole meuniére* on a menu that stays seasonal where possible.

The short-but-sweet beer list finds room for Maredsous 8 and La Chouffe on draught, plus five Trappists. One of the latter is the esteemed ■■ **Rochefort 8** (9.2%), a richly rounded chocolate brown ale that is almost as great as its double-digit sister, but less likely to induce unconsciousness.

38 Café Cantina De Groene Olifant 🍷

Sarphatistraat 510

T 020 620 4904

E info@degroeneolifant.demon.nl

www.degroeneolifant.nl

🕐 Fr–Sa 11.00–02.00; others 11.00–01.00

🍸 17

🍽 Uitsmijters, soups, rolls, snacks, daily specials

🚋 9, 10, 14 (Alexanderplein)

East of Artis Zoo and close to the Tropenmuseum, the split-level 'Green Elephant' has a decidedly pachydermal slant in its décor. Paintings and busts adorn its walls, and wooden, marble, alabaster and porcelain tusked beasties line the shelf above the bar.

Allegedly you could once see the elephant house in the nearby zoo from here, though the name is more likely to come from the 1970s. A previous landlord had owned a bar in the red light district, where he commissioned a local artist to paint pink elephants on the walls. The artist had no pink paint, only green. When the landlord moved here he took the name with him. (The elephant house has also relocated. What you get instead are antelope. Still a pretty bizarre sight from a pub window in northern Europe.)

The main bar has a tiled floor with fairy lights. A wooden-floored seating area is a few steps up from there. The music was so quiet on our last visit we cannot tell you what was playing. Food is snacks by day, but a changing daily special becomes available in the evening.

The short beer list takes deviations off the norm including several from Slaghmuylder brewery, a family concern in East Flanders. Their brand names are easier to pronounce, such as ▌▌**Witkap Pater Dubbel** (7%), a bittersweet dark brown ale with a slightly burnt edge to it.

39 **De Haven van Texel**
Sint Olofsteeg 11
T 020 427 0768
www.havenvantexel.nl
⊗ Closed Monday & Tuesday
🕐 We–Su from 16.30
🍷 10
🍴 Dutch/International
🚆 Amsterdam CS

At the junction of two old canals, the 'Texel Harbour' has one of the best views of any café in the city, from its small waterside terrace, weather permitting.

It was not always as nice. This former "Scottish bar and brothel" used to sell McEwan's by the bucket and rent upstairs rooms by the half hour. Things have changed vastly in recent years as the fringes of the red light district have been cleaned up. A 'brew with a screw' has been transformed into a 'brew with a view'.

Nowadays, the split-level, wooden-floored café-restaurant plays easy listening music (think Sade and Dionne Warwicke), and has a menu that includes steak and spare ribs. The house speciality is Indonesian saté with a Dutch twist of huge

portions, though there is also *Texels Lam*, a sheep stew from the island that gives the place its name.

The Texel theme continues with most of the beers from the island's eponymous brewery. Quality has improved continually since it opened in 1999, the range including Skuumkoppe (or 'Foam Top'), the Netherlands' first top-fermented, dark wheat beer. Our recommendation is ▬ **Texels Dubbel** (6.4%), the draught unfiltered, ruby-brown dubbel – pleasantly understated, rich in the mouth with a hint of sweetness, but without any cloying caramel edge. Ingredients include 'dune-filtered' water, malted island barley and the tranquil nature of the island influencing fermentation to improve flavours.

Café Heffer (& Ambassade, & Baantjer Museumcafé)
Oudebrugsteeg 7 & Warmoesstraat 66
T 020 428 4488
E info@heffer.nl
www.heffer.nl
Fr–Sa 10.00–03.00; others 10.00–01.00
15
Dutch/English
Amsterdam CS

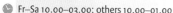

The former city assizes opened as a café in 1997 after major restoration. The Heffer on Oudebrugsteeg was the original 1637 court and now has sandy floors and an airy feel thanks to large windows, though canned Bonnie Tyler and friends can detract from its charm. Décor includes heavy cast iron high tables, and a bar counter with a lovely dark marble top.

Next door, the more spacious but virtually windowless Ambassade opened in 2007. Its modern interior has polished dark wood and mirrors everywhere, a large video screen at the back and church pew seating lining two walls. Stools are dotted around high tables. Above the bar is a portrait of AC Baantjer, former policeman and novelist who set his detective books in this vicinity. His lead character, Inspector De Kok, is the Dutch Inspector Morse.

The food (Anglo-Dutch fare including English breakfasts, and even fish and chips with malt vinegar) and drinks menu is the same in both.

The beer list is from owners, Lindedoom, a brewery based in Dutch Limburg. They brew the palatable **Venloosch Alt** (4.5%), available here on draught. It is light amber, dryish, and has a very slight hint of bitterness in the aftertaste. It was also the first Dutch Düsseldorf-style altbier.

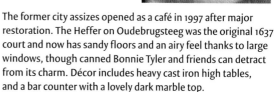

⓸ Café Hegeraad 🍷
Noordermarkt 84
T 020 624 5565
Daily 09.00–01.00
🍸 6
🍴 Snacks, hard-boiled eggs, croissants, rolls, soup
🚌 Stop/Go (Noordermarkt)

The Hegeraad is a timeless brown café in the Jordaan, occupying a cramped warren of three rooms. It has leaded glass windows, ancient wallpaper, wood panelling and (yes!) carpets on the tables worn threadbare by decades of elbows. There is no music, only conversation, often loud and enthusiastic.

There are ancient stone jenever barrels above the counter in the front bar. The central sitting room is replete with a grandfather clock, a glorious oak-beamed ceiling and a painting so darkened that only the contours of the canvas can be seen. The rear room, with its tatty wood ceiling is no less wonderful. On Saturday, the market on the square outside means it can be standing room only.

Note the tiny pissoir in the main room – a wee cupboard in every sense – has an inside window and a metal plate with holes drilled through for ventilation. For the more sensitive, there are real toilets downstairs.

The beer list is short but considered. The house pils is Pilsener Urquell, the markedly superior Czech original. Our choice however, is ▌▌**Watou's Witbier** (5%), from the Van Eecke brewery in West Flanders. Cloudy and refreshing, with citrus hints in the background and no sweetness, it is one of the best Belgian wheat beers.

Café Restaurant Hesp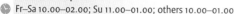
Weesperzijde 130–131
T 020 665 1202
E info@cafehesp.nl
www.cafehesp.nl
Fr–Sa 10.00–02.00; Su 11.00–01.00; others 10.00–01.00
24
Hamburgers, rolls, omelettes, full meals
M Wibautstraat
12 (Amstel Station or Amsteldijk)
Amsterdam Amstel

Beside the River Amstel, a few minutes' walk from Amstel station, this large café is off the beaten track but well worth finding. A wine and cognac vendor since 1890, it became a café in 1897 – the sepia-stained glass panel at the back commemorates its 50th anniversary in 1947.

Coloured leaded glass windows, rough wooden furniture, bare floorboards and nicotine-stained ceilings. It is split in two, barely perceptibly, with bar stools and standing room at the front, and tables at the rear for earnest, beer-fuelled political debate. Candle-lit for atmosphere, breweriana for beeriness and a trophy cabinet with photographs of neighbourhood sports teams for local credentials. There is a riverside terrace.

Good Dutch food covers soups and rolls at lunch to changing mains in the evening. There is also a surprisingly good wine list, including spectacular Italians such as Brunello, available by the glass.

Up to four of the 14 taps may host seasonal beers and there are a few 75cl bottles available too, with rare finds like Moinette Blonde. Their house beer, ■■ **Hesp Blond** (7.9%), is a sweetish strong blond ale with just a touch of bitterness. Marshmallow notes threaten to overpower at first but fade quickly. It is one of many beers produced to order by the Van Steenberge brewery in East Flanders.

Café Hoppe

Spui 18–20

T 020 420 4420

www.cafe-hoppe.nl

'Sitting Hoppe' daily from 08.00.
'Standing Hoppe' Fr–Su from 12.00; others from 14.00

16

Sandwiches, soups, snacks

1, 2, 5 (Spui)

This bipolar café has two bars so utterly different from each other that they would qualify as separate entities were it not for the unmarked sliding door behind the bar. Officially dubbed 'sitting Hoppe' and 'standing Hoppe', though they might be called 'young' and 'old' respectively, for both the décor and the demographics of the regulars.

If you are after the atmosphere of Old Amsterdam, join the gravel-voiced locals propping up the bar of the older, 'standing' room (which has seats).

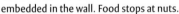

They have been serving customers here 1670, as suggested by the large oil painting, basic lighting from marvellously inadequate bulbs and candles, wooden wall benches and sand-strewn floor. Spirit barrels are embedded in the wall. Food stops at nuts.

The younger, 'sitting' part is less charming, has louder music, a grand café feel – and some standing room. This side is for couples on a date who care less about, and will not notice anyway, what and where they are drinking. There are a few snacks this side too.

Sadly the beer list is not quite as spectacular as the setting, but there are some good options. One is **Zatte** (8%), a golden unfiltered organic tripel, with a fruity aroma. This was the first beer created by the city's 't IJ brewery (see next entry) and has been popular ever since.

44 Brouwerij/Proeflokaal 't IJ

Funenkade 7

T 020 622 8325 (brewery); 020 320 1786 (café)
E info@brouwerijhetij.nl
www.brouwerijhetij.nl

Daily 15.00–20.00

7

Bar snacks

Tram 10 (Hoogte Kadijk) or 14 (Pontanusstraat)

The river IJ (say 'eye' and you are not far off) empties into the sea at Amsterdam. To find the simple but characterful brewpub named after it head East from the centre along the waterfront and aim at the much photographed windmill that is its neighbour.

The tiled walls are from the old bathhouse that used to occupy these premises. Its shelves are lined with beer bottles from the world over. The lampshades are ostrich eggs – because the company's logo is an ostrich and, allegedly, because IJ sounds a bit like *ei* (egg). The draping of dried hops hither and thither absorbs some of the smoke.

The café seems permanently busy during its limited opening hours – inside and out. Food means plates of cheese, salami, nuts and *ossenworst*.

The brewery's entire range is organic, unfiltered, unpasteurised and top-fermented. When it opened in 1985 it was in the vanguard of a welcome resurgence in Dutch craft brewing. Its output is a drop in the ocean compared to the likes of Heineken, but it brews more beer than them in Amsterdam.

This being the brewery tap, you can try all the beers straight from the tank, with seven typically available. The seasonal brews vary but ▦ **Plzen** (5%), a blond unfiltered ale, is available year-round. The only other city café where you will find it on draught is De Balie, just of Leidseplein, which narrowly missed our cut.

Despite bearing the Czech name for the town where blond lager was invented, this is a top-fermented beer, so not a true Pilsener, though it is its subtlety and flavour still challenges the factory-fed palates of local drinkers.

45 **Café de Jaren** 🍷 ⊗
Nieuwe Doelenstraat 20–22
T 020 625 5771
www.diningcity.nl/cafedejaren
Fr–Sa 09.30–02.00; others 09.30–01.00
16
Rolls, salads, pasta, soups (to 23.00), main meals (from 17.30)
4, 9, 16, 24, 25 (Muntplein)

The 'Years' is one of the city's largest cafés. Dating from 1990, it is an airy barn of a place with high ceilings and cream-coloured paint throughout. The only decorations are the art house posters on the supporting pillars carrying ads for films that even missed the cinegeeks.

It attracts arty and in-the-know Amsterdammers, who come to discuss Almodóvar's latest film or the new Kandinsky exhibition. Men drape loosely tied scarves round their necks even in high summer.

The well-stocked reading table usually includes today's British dailies, and American weekly stalwarts like *Time* and *Newsweek*. At the back, beyond the sea of blue-brown beige floor tiles on the floor that can send you bug-eyed if you stare, grand windows look out onto the junction of the Amstel river with the Kloveniersburgwal canal. In fine weather the large waterside terrace and equally ample one on the floor above get packed.

A reasonable selection of light meals is available downstairs, while the upstairs dining area is upmarket and evenings only, with more French influence on the menu.

The list is arty rather than beery, though there is enough to get your attention. ▪▪▪ **Struis** (9%) is another organic, unfiltered offering from 't IJ, a pleasant, chocolaty and not-too-sweet strong stout. Its name is Dutch for the ostrich that is the brewer's logo.

46 Muziek Café Restaurant Kapitein Zeppos
Gebed Zonder End 5
T 020 624 2057
E kapitein@zeppos.nl
www.zeppos.nl
Fr–Sa 12.00–03.00; others 12.00–01.00
13
Belgian
4, 9, 14, 16, 24, 25 (Spui/Rokin)

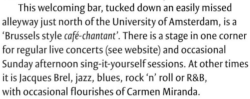

Kapitein Zeppos began life on 1960s Belgian TV as a fictional superhero, described as a cross between Batman and James Bond. The café that takes his name is about as un-Amsterdam as any in this book.

This welcoming bar, tucked down an easily missed alleyway just north of the University of Amsterdam, is a 'Brussels style *café-chantant*'. There is a stage in one corner for regular live concerts (see website) and occasional Sunday afternoon sing-it-yourself sessions. At other times it is Jacques Brel, jazz, blues, rock 'n' roll or R&B, with occasional flourishes of Carmen Miranda.

The Brussels connection runs to a full-sized but sadly unflowing Mannekin Pis, complete with bottom-revealing mirror. Tiled tables, climbing plants, wooden and mosaic-tiled floors. Paraphernalia include a bust of JFK, a miniature suit of armour, a Virgin Mary and a photograph of Senne Rouffaer, the actor who played Kapitein Zeppos.

Food is Belgian too, with shrimp croquettes and *moules frites*.

The only place the Brussels theme falls flat is the thin beer list, though hidden between the dull corporate brands is the draught version of ■■ **Blanche de Bruxelles** (4.5%), complete with its Mannekin Pis logo. This sweet, unfiltered wheat beer is so strongly honeyed you can almost hear the bees buzzing around the glass.

47 Kilimanjaro Afrikaans Restaurant
Rapenburgplein 6
T 020 622 3485
www.restaurantkilimanjaro.com
- Closed Monday
- Tu–Su 17.00–22.00
- 4
- Ethiopian & Pan-African
- 9, 14 (Mr Visserplein)
- 22, 42, 43 (Kadijksplein)

This small restaurant serves food from the length and breadth of a vast continent, from Moroccan *tajine* to South African *piri piri* prawns, via crocodile tail in mustard sauce from Senegal.

Our favourites are the Ethiopian *injeras*, vegetable dishes served on spongy flatbread the size of Frisbees, half-bread half-pancake, with or without spiced fish or meat. It serves as its own plate and cutlery – rip bits off and use them to scoop up the toppings.

Order the Ethiopian coffee at the end and it will be roasted there and then, filling the room with an unmistakable aroma. The cook may even bring the pan out for you to stick your nose in close and inhale deeply before she grinds the beans.

Backlit wall hangings have hand-painted African motifs. The floor is a chessboard of black and white tiles. The large map of Africa on the wall helps the geographically challenged figure out where their meal originated and of course, there is a photograph of Mount Kilimanjaro too.

The origin of ▪▪▪ **Abay Ethiopian Beer** (6.6%), despite its exotic name, is only a couple of streets away at De Prael.

Nonetheless, this amber ale is well-matched with the *injeras*. The malty nose, slightly sweet aroma, and bittersweet aftertaste of the liquid bread fits well with the more solid variety. It may not be genuinely Ethiopian but could you live with the guilt of all those food miles?

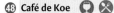

48 Café de Koe
Marnixstraat 381
T 020 625 44 82
E info@cafedekoe.nl
www.cafedekoe.nl

 Bar Sa–Su from 15.00; others from 16.00;
Restaurant daily 18.00–22.30

17

Bar snacks and full meals (restaurant only)

1, 2 or 5 (Leidseplein), or 7 (Raamplein)

Not far from Leidseplein, the 'Cow' is a split-level café-restaurant that splits as soon as you go through the door. Downstairs is for eating, upstairs for drinking, though this is not made obvious. The bar is split level too, a slightly raised area having a few tables that overlook the street.

If the aroma of garlic wafting up from the kitchen makes you hungry, the menu downstairs includes numerous, often cow-based hearty mains at reasonable prices.

The bovine theme stretches to several cow mosaics, inside and out, and a pair of longhorn horns centre stage behind the bar counter. You can make your own minds up about the rest of the 'Warholesque' art.

The music starts at loudish lounge/jazz/hip-hop and heads only one way from there. If you get bored, there are darts and a stack of board games.

The beer list includes several better Belgians and also the refreshingly fruity ▮▮**Boon Kriek** (4.5%), made by adding whole cherries to a young, light form of lambic. The use of whole fruit gives this entertaining drink the edge over most of its more commercial counterparts, which generally prefer to use industrially contrived syrups. Eminently drinkable, it has a nice balance of sour and sweet.

49 Café Koops 🐾
Damstraat 4
Haarlem
T 023 532 2760
E info@cafekoops.nl
www.cafekoops.nl
🕐 Fr–Sa 16.00–02.00; others 16.00–01.00
🍸 15
🍴 Tapas
🚌 300 (Centrum/Verwulft)

Opposite the corner St Bavo's cathedral, close to the Grote Markt and ten minutes' walk from Haarlem's station, time has stood still for a century at this little bar.

Its interior sits in permanent dusk. There are lights everywhere but they barely emit one candlepower each. The gloom and the gnarled surfaces of the old tabletops, worn over time into rippling ridges are only there to annoy beer writers attempting to record their thoughts on paper.

The light fittings hint at Art Deco, but the worn floorboards and mustard-coloured wall panels suggest something altogether older. Glass cabinets on the counter and the walls make this resemble more an old pharmacy than a café. Some contain porcelain and glass figurines.

Food is limited to pre-made tapas, though it is a miracle they get anything at all out the tiny kitchen. John Denver and country music fill the air, mercifully at low volume.

The beer taps jut from the wall behind the bar serving a selection that includes several from Haarlem's own Jopen brewery. Despite its name, **Jopen Hoppen** (6.8%) is not going to slap you round the face with the bitter hoppy vigour of an American-style IPA. Rather it is a pleasant, dry-hopped blond ale that starts out simple but develops evident hop flavours with time.

50 Eetcafé Kop van Jut
Leidsekruisstraat 24
T 020 320 7722
E info@kopvanjut.com
www.kopvanjut.com
Daily from 17.00
7
French-Dutch
1, 2, 5 (Leidseplein)

A Kop van Jut is a fairground 'test your strength' machine of the kind you whack with a mallet to make a bell ring and win a teddy. How that connects to this place, we have no idea.

Billing itself as an eetcafé (or bistro), in reality its cooking and ambiance suggest more a restaurant. It usually shuts once the last diners leave. The bar at the back doubles as a serving hatch for the open kitchen. They will only seat 36 diners and you may need to book ahead.

A typically vertiginous Amsterdam townhouse, it has steep stone

steps out front to trip up the unwary and an upstairs dining area reached only via a tight spiral staircase. Downstairs is so narrow in places that it can feel like dining in a corridor. However, generous portions of good French-influenced modern Dutch cuisine more than make up for any discomforts.

The walls are crammed with photos of Amsterdam celebs, and some questionable 7-inch vinyl singles. The latter include some best-forgotten attempts at musical stardom by sporting luminaries. Check out Marco van Basten and Frank Rijkaard duetting on *Het is Fijn in Italië te Zijn* (It's Great To Be in Italy). Or not, as you wish.

Besides one crowd-pleasing Pils the beers are exclusively produced locally by De Prael, including a house beer, **Kop van Jut Blond** (5.7%). This unfiltered blond ale is pleasantly well rounded, with a moderate strength, making it the ideal companion to any good meal.

51 Café Krom 🍷
Utrechtsestraat 76
T 020 624 5343
🕐 Fr–Sa 10.00–02.00; others 10.00–01.00
🍷 12
🍴 Snacks, toasted sandwiches, satay
🚌 Stop/Go (Utrechtsestraat)
🚊 4, 7, 10, 25 (Frederiksplein)

Utrechtsestraat is full of quirky bars and specialist stores, including the Netherlands' third-best cheese shop (yes, it's official) at No.90.

The 'Crooked' is an Art Deco cornershop café with marvellously eclectic decoration. The main table in the centre wears a thick carpet. A cabinet doubles as a shrine to local chanteuse Willeke Alberti, the 1960s Dutch answer to Petula Clark. In her dotage she has become a gay icon. She has also had a beer named after her by De Prael brewery, though ironically it is not available here.

The jukebox is stacked with tacky 70s classics and Dutch hits from all eras, most of which never crossed the North Sea. It is still operated using the bar's stock of old *kwartjes* (quarter guilder coins), which went out of circulation in 2001.

Food is limited and the satay actually comes from the Indonesian restaurant across the street. The menu lists many beers merely as 'dubbel', 'tripel' or 'witbier', suggesting they think their customers do not care who makes it. Even despite this, we like this place. The seasonal tap beer is usually the best option. On our last visit this was ▬ **Jopen Winterbier** (10%), a deep amber, bittersweet mouthful of contradictions with a malty nose – a warming seasonal brew for long dark northern European evenings.

52 Restaurant De Lieve
Herengracht 88
T 020 624 9635 (after 14.00)
E eten@restaurantlieve.nl
www.restaurantlieve.nl
Daily from 17.30
35
Belgian
1, 2, 5 (Nieuwezijds Kolk)

There are too few restaurants where beer and wine are accorded equal status. At the 'Beloved' each dish has a recommended brew to match with it. One would expect no less from a current and past holder of the national 'Beer and Gastronomy' award.

Grandiose and opulent, like a courtesan's boudoir with dining tables, the décor nudges surreal. A triptych of Adam and Eve surrounding the Virgin Mary on one wall sits next to Chinese-style wallpaper showing an Ardennes hunting scene replete with running wild boar.

The menu is proper Belgian – no cornball image of mussels 'n' chips served by waiters dressed as monks here. Choose between the conventional three-course 'Living Room' menu, a five-course 'Gastronomic' or the 'Baroque', a kind of Belgian mezze made up of three cold starters, four hot mains and three desserts, designed for sharing between two. All three feature dishes prepared with finesse using fresh seasonal ingredients, some cooked with beer, such as 'Maredsoep' (mushroom soup with Maredsous 8).

The beers are exclusively Belgian and you may want to opt for the 'beer arrangement', whereby a different brew is brought with each course without you having to specify. If we were to recommend just one brand here it would be **Karmeliet Tripel** (8.5%) from the Bosteels brewery. Its multi-grain recipe helps to create a rounded, not-too-dry, not-too-sweet blond ale that can be matched with most things and appeals to almost everyone.

If you want to move on to Dutch beers the Arendsnest (above) is next door.

Lokaal 't Loosje
Nieuwmarkt 32–34
T 020 627 2635
Fr–Sa 09.30–02.00; others 09.30–01.00
26
Breakfast, salads, sandwiches, snacks, soups, bagels
M Nieuwmarkt

The front bar of this delightful café has white tiles decorated with colourful tableaux from the 1930s, the most striking, taking up an entire wall, showing the Zuid Hollandsche Bierbrouwerij (ZHB), based in Den Haag (The Hague) and once one of the largest breweries in South Holland, before its closure in 1974.

The nicotine-yellowed walls of the raised area at the back are covered with black and white fading wedding photos, all seeming to date from the same pre-war period as the tableaux. The mirror may well be an original feature too, as it does not do a whole lot of reflecting any more. Great for atmosphere but not much good for narcissists or combing your hair.

Friendly and relaxed, feeling modern despite its age, it is one of the best drinking holes around Nieuwmarkt. In warmer weather the outdoor terrace is great for people-watching.

Food is simple but good. Large, good value breakfasts with toast, scrambled eggs, juice, coffee/tea, cheese, ham and trimmings. Beer, if you must, is extra. Ciabattas and bagels served later in the day are a cut above standard too.

The beers include La Chouffe and De Koninck on tap, as well as several in bottles from 't IJ.

■■ **Duchesse de Bourgogne** (6.2%), from the Verhaeghe brewery in West Flanders, is a fine reddish-brown oak-aged ale that has a strong sweet 'n' sour nose that tends to almost kriek-like sourness in the drinking.

54 **Café Luxembourg**
Spui 24
T 020 620 6264
E cafe@luxembourg.nl
www.luxembourg.nl
Fr–Sa 09.00–02.00; others 09.00–01.00
19
Breakfast, pasta, soups, salads, rolls, full meals
Tram 1, 2, 5 (Spui)

The Luxembourg could lay claim to being the second grandest café in town. The large conservatory at the front is perfect for ogling passers by. At the back, a crystal chandelier hangs above a raised area that looks out over the Singel canal. Art Deco ceiling lights bathe the whole in a warm glow after dark.

The theme is, well Luxembourg, though they cannot seem to decide whether this means the country (coat of arms is on the door), or the gardens (large b&w photos of bygone Paris). It is probably the former. The white-aproned staff are friendly and not nearly supercilious enough to be Parisian waiters.

The daytime menu is big-time brasserie and as broad and varied as you would expect from a place this size. You can get Eggs Benedict for breakfast (09.00–12.00).

It is a shame that such decadent surrounds are let down by a dull corporate beer list. We recommend you stick with the tap reserved for seasonal brews.

On our last visit this was **Affligem Christmas** (9%), a typically rich, dark red winter ale. Even though Affligem has been owned by Heineken since 2005, its beers have thus far retained small brewery excellence. This one has a strong caramel hit on the nose and is on the sweet side but is really quite palatable in small doses.

⑤⑤ Café het Melkwoud 🍷
Zijlstraat 63, Haarlem
T 023 574 9112
www.melkwoud.nl
Daily from 16.00
+/-30
None (we think)
Haarlem

The 'Milk Wood' is named after Dylan Thomas's play for voices, *Under Milk Wood*, broadcast on Dutch radio around the time the bar opened in 1968. Its sign – tree branches growing out of an ample female torso – comes from the cover of the first Dutch translation. However this is no Sailors Arms, but rather a dark brown Dutch café.

Ceiling murals aged and darkened by decades of smoke could be from Tolkein or the Brothers Grimm and seem to feature trolls, though we guess is they are meant to feature scenes from a day in the life of Gwalia.

On a busy shopping street, a hundred meters from the Grote Markt, it maintains a local atmosphere, with regulars on stools lining the bar from opening time. Loud rock and dim lighting give it a nocturnal feel even in the afternoon. Large windows help you see out but not in.

Among the dozen taps is **🟦 Pauwel Kwak** (8%), usually known as Kwak and famed for its glass. The 'coachman' is a round-bottomed vessel resembling a mini yard of ale, set on a wooden stand. Kwak was an innkeeper in Napoleonic Belgium who coaxed business out of passing stage coaches by designing a glass that could slot onto the side of the coach to assist spillage-free drinking-driving. The beer is toffee-coloured and sweet, the latter masking its high alcohol content, which in turn helps you feel less of a tit when drinking from such a container.

56 Mitra
Middenweg 57a
T 020 692 3658
www.mitra.nl
Closed Sunday
Mo 11.00–18.00; Tu–Fr 09.00–18.00; Sa 09.00–17.00
140
None
9 (Hogeweg)

Mitra is the Netherlands' second-largest off-licence chain, with around 300 branches nationwide. Local operators have some leeway over what they buy in, so some are great stores for beer lovers. One in Eindhoven has more than 600 different varieties. Most others fall short of the dizzying heights though there should be interesting options in all of them.

Of Amsterdam's seven Mitras, the widest selection is found in this corner shop on Middenweg in southeast Amsterdam, conveniently close to Elsa's (above). Opened in 2007, the friendly boss and his wife are beer enthusiasts and always on the lookout for new things.

You will find the beers towards the far corner as you enter, arranged by style: dubbel, tripel, wheat beers, fruit beers and so on. This means two from the same brewery may be some distance apart. Regulars include brews from Texel, Urthel, het Anker, Van Eecke, Halve Maan, Boon and St Bernard.

Texels Tripel (8.5%) is an unfiltered strong golden yellow ale made using barley grown on the island where the brewery is located. Finely balanced with just a hint of bitterness, it is one of the Netherlands's best attempts at the 'abbey tripel' style, and continues to improve year on year.

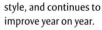

Two other Amsterdam Mitras worth noting if you are in the area, each with a beer list running to around 125 are at Rijnstraat 103 and Beukenweg 12.

⑤⑦ Old Nickel Hotel 🍷 🥨

Nieuwe Brugsteeg 11

T 020 624 1912

E info@oldnickel.nl

www.oldquarter.com/oldnickel

🍷 Daily 09.00–04.00

🍷 60+

🍴 Breakfast (hotel guests only)

🚆 Amsterdam CS

When the Old Nickel is empty it is a curiously appealing dive. When it is full it becomes charming, a tavern complete with wood panelling from the captain's cabin of a 17th century Dutch warship, a Delft tiled fireplace and a great beer selection.

Pino, the pub cat, is inconsistent too. Sometimes aloof and indifferent, on one visit he brazenly strolled over, leapt up and promptly fell asleep on the author's lap, purring contentedly through two complete rounds.

There is a hotel above with cheap rooms, no lift, steep stairs and shared bathrooms. Popular with single men on stag weekends, it is often noisy at night, though if you are one of those making the noise, it is a bargain, the price including a cooked breakfast to soak up the previous night's excesses.

There may be live music, with a jazz trio playing an impromptu set by the door.

About half the beers are Belgian – the others being mostly Dutch or German. Of the latter, ▰ **Aecht Schlenkerla Rauchbier** (5.1%) is one of the world's most unusual lagers, brewed with malt that has been richly smoked over beechwood, lending it an intense flavour. There are other smoked beers in the world but we have yet to try one that surpasses this Bamberg speciality. We adore it and find it manna from heaven, though there are some who see it as merely a liquid form of smoky bacon crisps.

58 In de Olofspoort
Nieuwe Brugsteeg 13
T 020 624 3918
E olofspoort@upcmail.nl
www.olofspoort.com
⊗ Closed Su–We (except for group bookings) and 4 weeks in summer
Th–Fr 17.00–00.00; Sa 16.00–00.00
3
Bar snacks
Amsterdam CS

With leaded windows, wooden ceilings, light-green-painted wooden walls, and every inch of shelving lined with stone bottles, this tasting room oozes history – though it has only had this function since 1988. It is built on the site of Sint Olofspoort, a city gate built in 1341 and named after St Olof to honour the Norwegian sailors who brought the trees from Scandinavia that under-pinned Amsterdam and prevented it sinking into the marsh.

The gate was demolished in 1618, and what is now the front room appeared a year later and for several centuries functioned as a bakery. There is no room to swing a cat. Not even an amputee. The back room, a little more private, is a bit larger.

The pleasing lack of music makes this a quiet haven in the midst of a district bustling with nightlife.

But if silence and chat aren't enough, on the third Tuesday of odd-numbered months there's a 'singalong' at 19.30. Don't say we didn't warn you. They're also licensed as a wedding venue if you fancy tying the knot in a pub.

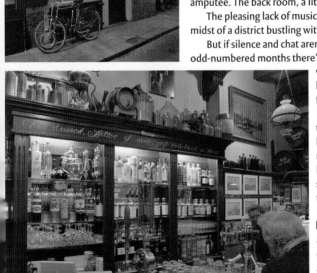

The beer list is rubbish, but this is forgivable as there are two hundred other drinks on the menu, including rare jenevers, liqueurs and an array of flavoured spirits in bottles made to make them seem ancient.

Of the beers we recommend **Affligem Dubbel** (6.8%), another from the Heineken-owned, small Belgian ale brewery. An unchallenging dark brown ale that is unlikely to win any independent awards, it is a perfectly decent session brew.

59 Café Onder de Ooievaar

Utrechtsestraat 119

T 020 624 6836

www.onderdeooievaar.nl

Fr–Sa 10.00–03.00; Su 10.30–01.00; others 10.00–01.00

26

Toasted sandwiches, snacks, rolls, salads, omelettes, uitsmijters

BUS Stop/Go (Utrechtsestraat)

Tram 4, 7, 10, 25 (Frederiksplein)

This corner café with large shop windows looks out onto the Prinsengracht canal as it passes under bustling Utrechtsestraat. Though unpromising from the outside, wooden floors, well-worn furnishings and a nicotine-scarred ceiling give it a cosy lived-in feel of an easy-going neighbourhood bar.

Its summer terrace lets you watch the human traffic pass over and under the adjacent bridge, and the brisk business of the flower stall by day. Red-cushioned stools line the bar. An unexplained collection of antique spoons hangs in the corner.

We like to think it is called 'Under the Stork' because you will find birds on the roof in the nesting season, though we doubt it. Bob the house tabby had his 15th birthday party in April 2010 and is often seen lying around.

Food (from 17.30) is Dutch pub grub, though the rolls and toasted sandwiches are above average. Try the gorgonzola and pear, or chicken satay toasties, or the beef carpaccio roll with pine nuts, parmesan, rocket and pesto.

The beer menu also deviates from the norm. ■■ **Gouden Carolus Classic** (8%), from the Anker brewery in Mechelen, Belgium is a dark brown sturdy delight and the original Gouden Carolus brand, though numerous others have been spawned in recent years. Still the best of a good bunch, it demands your attention. Its quality seems to get better and better.

Proeflokaal de Ooievaar

Sint Olofspoort 1

T 020 420 8004

www.proeflokaaldeooievaar.nl

Daily from 12.00

6

Boiled eggs

Amsterdam CS

'The Stork' is another of that top notch cluster of bars at the station end of Zeedijk. A jenever tasting room since 1782, beer has taken a bit more prominence in recent years. Stone steins hang from the ceiling, antique tiles cover one wall, and there is wood panelling on the others.

The beer taps are embedded in the tiles behind the impressive wooden bar counter, and bare floorboards betray the wear marks of age. Its tiny single room has space for a only a handful of tables. It is pretty popular, so come early if you want a seat. Conversation is lively, assisted by the absence of music.

The cramped layout means the steep steps down to the loo involve a careful risk analysis. The food menu is a classic too – hard-boiled eggs with salt and pepper, only. Here the cat is Tijger, a swaggerer who once walked between the legs of a police horse.

There are plenty of jenevers and other spirits to try. The Ooievaar brands are produced by the van Wees family, who also run the Admiraal (above).

There are only six beers and all are dispensed on draft, including Gouden Carolus Classic and the house special, **Ooievaar Bier** (7.5%), an unfiltered tripel brewed to order just down the way by De Prael (below). Its initial sweetness fades, the further down the glass you head.

 Café Oosterling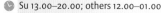
Utrechtsestraat 140
T 020 623 4140
Su 13.00–20.00; others 12.00–01.00
14
Snacks, tapas, nachos
Stop/Go (Utrechtsestraat)
4, 7, 10, 25 (Frederiksplein)

The Oosterling has been a bar and off-licence since 1820, since when the inside has changed little but for the bonsai microwave and the TV. The building dates from 1735 and was originally used by the Dutch East India Company to sell coffee, tea and spices. The current owners are only the fourth generation of the Oosterling family to run it since they took over in 1879.

On a busy junction at the south end of Utrechtsestraat, a traffic light almost bars your exit, not that leaving is a priority. In 2010 the Dutch restaurant and catering association voted this the Netherlands' no. 2 café.

The bar counter is bizarrely low, and the stools have been truncated to compensate. And no it isn't you, the building really does list a bit, as does the mosaic floor. It is an uphill walk from the barrel tables by the window to the bar and the rack of giant casks, once used to store drinks for off sales.

This is a place to come for a casual chat. There is no music, except the random chiming of the clock. It tells the right time but can strike at nine minutes to the hour.

A classic brew equal to these magnificent surroundings is ▮▮ **Orval** (6.2%), the Trappist beer that resembles no other in style or taste. A golden amber, heavily dry-hopped ale, it pokes your palate every time you sip but avoids deep-set bitterness to become delightfully moreish.

62 De Pilsener Club
Begijnensteeg 4
T 020 623 1777
Closed Sunday
Fr–Sa 12.00–02.00; Mo–Th 12.00–01.00
23
Hot dogs, snacks, toasted sandwiches
1, 2, 4, 5, 9, 14, 16, 24, 25 (Spui)

Although the sign on the door says Pilsener Club, this extraordinary one-room café with sand-strewn wooden floors is widely known as De Engelse Reet, meaning 'the English alleyway' because the English Reformed Church is there. It is translated by many guidebooks as 'the English Arse' for reasons of right on, eye-catching gullibility.

This is another interior that looks as if it has not changed in a century – the peeling, smoke-blackened wallpaper certainly hasn't. There is no bar as such, just a door at the back through which the landlord arrives with fresh supplies.

The clock at the back is permanently 15 minutes fast. Brass plaques by some tables commemorate the spots where now-departed locals once made their home-from-home for many years. The walls are hung with paintings of Amsterdam, though

pride of place goes to a large portrait of a St Bernard dog.

A dark bar like this deserves a dark beer, and they don't come any blacker than **Van Vollenhoven Extra Stout** (7%). Formally a big brewery brand, it disappeared a decade ago, but has been revived by De Schans in Uithoorn, as part of the revival of Dutch stout brewing. Stronger than average, it is chocolaty, bitter and dry. It is available here on draught and in bottle, the former being drier with more bitter cocoa, while the latter has a darker head and veers more towards coffee than chocolate.

⑥ De Prael Proeflokaal & Brouwerij 🍷 🏪 🍺

Warmoesstraat 15 (café); Oudezijds Voorburgwal 30 (brewery & shop)

T 020 408 4470 (brewery & shop) **E** info@deprael.nl

www.deprael.nl

🕐 *Brewery*: Mo–Fr 09.00–16.30
    Shop: Mo 12.30–17.00; Th 10.00–21.00; Sa &Su 12.00–18.00; others 10.00–18.00
    Café: Shut Monday & Tuesday; others 15.00–20.00

🍸 8 (café) / 30 (shop)

🍴 Bar snacks, daily special (café), cheese (shop)

🚆 Amsterdam CS

The 'Pearl' began life in 2002 as the brainchild of two friends, one of whom was a social worker intent on giving work experience to people with learning disabilities. All their beers are named after famous local crooners. Tours, tastings and 'brew yourself' days can be arranged. The shop also stocks around 25 brews from other small Dutch independents, plus organic cheese made using Willy and André beer

The current tap is 200 metres away around the corner but will move alongside the brewery by 2011. This atmospheric wooden-floored café with old album covers on its walls, and a dozen different types of lampshade is set to expand its opening hours. It sells all the available beers with a selection of 'amuse-bouche' celebrations of Dutch cuisine.

The brewery produces eight beers, some seasonal, with five or six available at any time. The numbers are topped up with guests from other Dutch independents, often served from wooden casks.

Given its location in the Red Light District, it would be remiss of us not to recommend their strong ale, ▄▄▄ **Willy** (11%). This dark brown heavyweight has a spicy nose, hints of banana and chocolate, and a slight bitterness in the aftertaste. If it is not available, try a **Johnny** instead.

64 Café de Roemer
Botermarkt 17, Haarlem
T 023 532 5267
www.cafederoemer.nl
Daily from 11.00
32
Soups, salads, rolls (lunch); full meals (evening) –
Dutch/international
 Haarlem, then Bus 300 (Centrum/Verwulft)

There are five hostelries in a row on Haarlem's most popular square for outdoor drinking and this has the best beer list. De Gooth next door and the Linde at no.21 have the next best. Wide terraces compete for customers on warmer days and a bar crawl could literally be done on hands and knees.

A 'roemer' is a 'rummer' – a bowl-shaped glass, often engraved, used for drinking toasts, popular round these parts in the 16th and 17th centuries and also found in the UK, where the word derives from the Dutch.

An inner terrace within a glass conservatory functions when the weather does not co-operate. The Art Deco interior is larger than it appears from outside, opening out at the back into a wide seating area. The centrepiece is a coloured glass frieze behind the bar depicting a minstrel and dancer.

The beer list includes the full range from Jopen, Karmeliet and several Trappists, including most from Schaapskooi abbey, currently the only Trappist brewery outside Belgium. Throughout Europe their beers are usually sold under the brand name of La Trappe – though they are called Koningshoeven in North America. Their blue riband product is arguably **La Trappe Tripel** (8%), an uncomplicated strong golden blond ale that is deceptive in its drinkability thanks in part to background hints of coriander.

⑥⑤ Café Schiller 🍷 ✖

Rembrandtplein 24a

T 020 624 9846

E info@cafeschiller.nl

www.cafeschiller.nl

🕐 Fr 16.00–03.00; Sa 13.00–03.00; Su 13.00–01.00; others 16.00–01.00

🍷 16

🍴 Snacks (all day), bar meals & French (dinner only)

🚊 4, 9 & 14 (Rembrantplein)

Next to the NH hotel of the same name, the Schiller has been a meeting place for the glitterati since it opened in 1913. From the outside it looks like the dingiest and least appealing of the numerous joints on or around popular Rembrandtplein, but in our opinion is the best.

The covered patio at the front has to be the only carpeted terrace in Amsterdam. Beyond, another world awaits. This is a fabulous Art Deco café, with marble walls, subdued lighting, and green and white striped seating, glass mosaics, period paintings and objets d'art, all reflecting its 1920s heyday.

Some paintings are by artist and former owner Frits Schiller, after whose father Georg the café is named. The tiled mural is of a Pierrot and accompanying itinerant musicians. We like the two lobsters painted on the light above the bar. Billie Holiday, Louis Armstrong and Frank Sinatra enhance the ambiance.

By comparison, the carpeted, low-ceilinged rear room – which becomes the restaurant in the evening – is strangely ordinary. This does not stop a cornucopia

of French delights, from oysters and lobster, through steak tartare, turbot and *cassoulet*, to crème brûlée. For simpler dining the bar has a daily changing selection of mains.

While the tap beers are largely forgettable, more than half the short bottled range comes from 't IJ, whose ▦ **Columbus** (9%) is a satisfying sweet-but-not-too-sweet, dark amber brew that is full and rich in the mouth. Like all the IJ products, it's organic.

66 Schuim
Spuistraat 189
T 020 638 9357
Fr–Sa 11.00–02.00; others 11.00–01.00
20
Toasted sandwiches, pasta, soup, salads, main meals
1, 2, 5, 9, 13, 14, 16, 17, 24, 25 (Dam Square)

A couple of minutes' walk from Dam Square, the 'Foam' is a fashionable café with warped wooden floorboards and a circle of tiles in the middle, as if the designers could not make up their mind. The colourful room is lit by an eclectic collection of lamps from a Medusa-like candelabra to a swarm of flying saucers from a 1950s B-movie Martian invasion.

Two walls are covered with loud, brightest abstract mural – a kind of leaded-glass-effect, sub-Picasso sea of eyes and noses in any colour bar subtle. Not recommended if hung over. Officially an art gallery, on several visits we have yet to see artworks beyond these permanent decorations.

Table service is slow to non-existent so go the British way direct from the bar. The music (modern R&B) gets louder as the evening progresses. Food runs the full range of safe Dutch café stuff, including good homemade burgers.

The beer menu is not as colourful as the walls, but throws in a few pleasing curve balls. Best of the bunch is the undersung classic **Witkap Pater Stimulo** (6%), a pale golden top-fermented blond produced by the Slaghmuylder family in Belgian East Flanders. Less spectacularly dry than it once was, it remains full of character and promise. A decidedly superior fermented barley drink.

⑥⑦ Café de Sluyswacht
Jodenbreestraat 1
T 020 625 7611
E info@sluyswacht.nl
www.sluyswacht.nl

🍷 Fr–Sa 11.30–03.00; Su 11.30–19.00; others 11.30–01.00
🍸 9
🍴 Snacks and toasted sandwiches
Ⓜ Nieuwmarkt or Waterlooplein
🚊 9, 14 (Waterlooplein)

Do not adjust your vision. This canalside café, just steps from the Rembrandthuis, leans heavily to starboard. The adjacent St Anthonius lock was installed in 1602 to keep the water in the canals at the right level and prevented enemy ships sailing in. This former home for the lock keeper (Du: *sluyswacht*) was added in 1695.

Set back a little from the road, the canalside terrace is one of the cutest in town.

The house was derelict for many years and only opened for business a decade ago after major restoration, though it feels like an ancient pub. There are tiled floors, green walls and hard wooden benches that leave your backside complaining if you linger too long. A map of Old Amsterdam shows how the city looked before it broke out beyond its canal belt. A ship's light and bell by the bar add a nautical theme. There are more tables on the first floor.

There is no room for them to cook more than basic snacks, nor to store more than a short range of beers.

One beer that is in stock is ▮▮ **La Chouffe** (8%), often on tap. This coriander-laced golden ale is less complex on draught than from the bottle but remains one for which the term 'quaffable' was invented. It became part of Duvel Moortgat in 2006, although it's still brewed at the Achouffe brewery in the far south of the Belgian Ardennes.

68 Café 't Smalle 🍷 ❌
Egelantiersgracht 12
T 020 623 9617
E cafe.t.smalle@gmail.com
www.t-smalle.nl
🕐 Fr–Sa 10.00–02.00; others 10.00–01.00
🍸 20+
🍴 Salads, rolls, lunches
🚌 Stop/Go (Egelantiersgracht)

The beautiful 'Narrow' café, in the fashionable Jordaan district is where Pieter Hoppe started his first distillery in 1780. Just outside the inner ring of canals, it became a café in 1978, retaining several original elements, transporting you back in time and making it one of the most charismatic places in Amsterdam.

The high-ceilinged bar has tiled floors, leaded glass windows and a giant candelabra. Behind the wooden serving counter is a pyramid of jenever barrels. At the rear of the room is a short wooden spiral staircase leading up to a cosy mezzanine with wood-panelled walls and creaky chairs. A glass panel on one side looks back down to the main bar. Candles on the tables add to the atmosphere.

Food is tasty and good value, though erring on the safe side. Like many of the best places, it has no music. And as befits an old building the walls lean a bit, we think, though it could be the beer affecting perception. As soon as the weather is warm enough, a small canalside terrace becomes the focus of attention – though space is at a premium here.

🟦🟥 **Gouden Carolus Tripel** (9%), from Het Anker in Mechelen, Belgium, is a dry, well-rounded strong blond ale. The refined and restrained balance of hops and fruity notes, along with quite subtle sweetness all hide the alcohol content well, so approach with care.

69 Spuyt

69 **Café de Spuyt**
Korte Leidsedwarsstraat 86
T 020 624 8901
E info@cafedespuyt.nl
www.cafedespuyt.nl
Daily from 16.00
100+
Snacks, toasted sandwiches
1, 2, 5 (Leidseplein)

One of Amsterdam's better-kept secrets, this cracker of a specialist beer café should not be missed. Open since 1968, in the last few years the landlord made the decision to send it beery, edging the range up into three figures. Beer tasting evenings are held every third Monday of the month from 20.15.

A few steps from the bright lights of Leidseplein, but seven leagues distance in terms of atmosphere, visiting this friendly one-room joint feels a bit like popping into someone's front room to share a brew. Unassuming from the outside and easily walked past, it has a long banquette down one side, plus basic wooden high tables and stools.

The beer list on the wall is a joy to read, with numerous favourites and a fine selection of Belgian and Dutch stalwarts. The house's signature beer comes however from the beer belt of northern France and is a classic, though it can be so elusive that supplies are sometimes interrupted.

Share a 75cl cork-topped bottle of **Trois Monts** (8.5%) to understand what is meant by the phrase, "Great French beer". The Brasserie St Sylvestre is in French Flanders, between Calais and Lille. The three hills in question are the ones around the Flemish town of Ieper (Fr: *Ypres*) that saw heavy fighting during the 1914–18 War.

This dryish golden ale has a fine balance of fruit and hoppy bitterness. Termed a '*bière de garde*', or stored beer, it is matured in cellars over the colder months in the same vein as a Wallonian saison.

70 Café-restaurant Star Ferry

Piet Heinkade 1

T 020 788 2090 (café)

E reserveringen@starferry.nl

www.starferry.nl

Daily 10.30–23.00 (open until 00.00 on performance nights)

13

Snacks, fruit tarts, sandwiches, uitsmijters, soups, salads, mains

Amsterdam CS

25, 26 (Muziekgebouw Bimhuis)

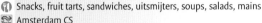
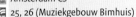

Only five minutes' walk from the station, Amsterdam's spectacular, glass-fronted concert hall, the Muziekgebouw aan het IJ, opened on the waterfront in 2005. It hosts all kinds of art events – check via **www.muziekgebouw.nl**. This multiple prize-winning building was the brainchild of Danish architects 3xN. The Star Ferry is its main café.

Arriving by tram or on foot, the entrance is across a bridge at second floor level. The café is on the ground floor and is accessible to all. You come to the Star Ferry for its spectacular location and exceptional design. High-ceilinged, two of its glass walls look out across the river, to the ferries scuttling back and forth to north Amsterdam. Light wood furnishings keep everything sleek and Scandinavian.

The food menu is reasonably priced, snacks including falafels and goats' cheese croquettes. There are also three daily specials – one fish, one meat, one veggie. For jazz, take the lift to the third floor for the Bimhuis jazz club (**bimhuis.nl**) and another bar, daily from 18.30.

Gerardus Wittems Kloosterbier Dubbel (7%) comes from the long-established Gulpener brewery in the deep south of Limburg, near the Belgian border. This dark reddish-brown ale is arguably the brewery's best, and a lot less caramel-sweet than most Dutch dubbels. Instead it has touch of sourness, even a hint of cocoa in the slightly bitter aftertaste.

71 Studio

71 Café Studio
Grote Markt 25, Haarlem
T 023 531 0033
E info@cafestudio.nl
www.cafestudio.nl
Fr 12.00–03.00; Sa 11.00–03.00; Su 11.00–02.00;
others 12.00–02.00
40
Paninis (lunch only), snacks
Haarlem

On Haarlem's main square, this former cinema is now one of the city's largest and most popular cafés, treading a fine line between sophisticated and garish. A large canopy light covers much of a ceiling with Art Deco aspirations, and there are tulips on the tables. A raised area at the back doubles as a stage when needed, overlooked by a crystal chandelier and backed by a green velvet curtain.

Civilised by day, in the late evening industrial strength music will keep you and the rest of the city awake, as the place gets packed with young people trying to become romantically acquainted on the dance floor, without the use of conversation. There are live DJs at weekends, when another room upstairs opens to cope with peak loads. Come early to avoid tinnitus.

Some of the beer taps change with the seasons and even during nightclub hours always feature something of interest, with good representation from Haarlem's Jopen brewery, a couple from SNAB and a fair selection of Trappists.

'Bruges Fool', or **Brugse Zot Blond** (6%) is a delicate golden blond ale that is perhaps a little too easy to drink, though it develops more allure as the years pass. Introduced in 2005 to relaunch family brewing at the Halve Maan brewery in Bruges, which had been largely dormant for several years, it has proved hugely successful.

Riviervischmarkt 13, Haarlem

T 023 532 5399

E info@indenuiver.nl

www.indenuiver.nl

Fr–Sa 14.00–04.00; Su 14.00–02.00; others 16.00–02.00

25

Snacks

Haarlem

When owner Paul took on this captivating three-roomed Haarlem café close to the Grote Markt in 1997, he was determined get it voted the best in the country. It came fourth in 2010.

The front bar is decorated with Delft tiles and has beer taps embedded in a marble wall. The central room has olive-painted wooden walls and gas lamp lighting. The aeronautical theme – model planes, airline baseball caps and a cabinet of Delftware airline crockery – honours Haarlem's aviation pioneer Anthony Fokker, whose aircraft dominated the market between the wars.

The *Uiver* was a Douglas DC-2, assembled by Fokker for KLM, which found its place in Dutch history by winning its class in the 1934 Melbourne Race. Ironically this success meant Fokker lost out to Douglas as KLM's preferred supplier, despite the original plane crashing in 1935.

The third area is a snug, leather-walled room, rescued from the offices of the *Haarlemse Dagblad*, the world's oldest newspaper still in print, continuously since 1656, and the second oldest paper.

To mark the fact this was until 1981 a fishmonger's, free herring is handed round on Saturdays. Restrained live music on Thursday and Sunday, plus some Saturdays, may involve for example a pianist.

As well as a couple of dozen beers, the drinks menu includes 50 whiskies and 30 jenevers. Such a local-themed pub demands a local brew and we recommend the town's own **Jopen Koyt** (8%), an accomplished dark brown ale pitched somewhere around a strong dubbel.

73 Café Vertigo
Vondelpark 3
T 020 612 3021
www.vertigo.nl
Sa–Su 10.00–01.00; others 11.00–01.00
16
Pasta, burger, satay, snacks, rolls, salads
1 (1e Constantijn Huygensstraat)

Vertigo occupies the white vaulted cellar of the pavilion – home of the national Film Museum – in the northeast corner of the city's main lung, Vondelpark. One wall of the main bar is littered with photos of movie stars through the ages. Not all are old, as witnessed by a still shot from 2009's *Inglourious Basterds*.

The area at the rear has even bigger photos, dominated by a huge iconic restaurant scene from Brian De Palma's 1987 classic *The Untouchables*.

Low lighting and candlelit tables create a convivial, romantic air throughout, assisted by music that knows the meaning of background.

The gigantic terrace has chairs, tables and even a few throw pillows, plus grand views of the museum on one side, and the leafy park with duck-strewn pond on the other. If eating *al fresco* keep an eye out for the cocky pigeons, adept at stealing pieces of ciabatta. The impressive doorstop sandwiches are literally a cut above the crowd – chicken, bacon, roast aubergine, rocket and mayo is a favourite.

The corporate-dominated beer list unravels a bit, but a few are up to the scenery. Antwerp's own reddish-brown, dryish pale ale, **De Koninck** (5%) may appear ordinary on the surface, but packs in as much complexity as many beers twice its strength. It is one of those consistently good lighter brews that has stayed the distance without lowering its standards in response to simpler demands.

74 In de Waag
Nieuwmarkt 4
T 020 422 7772
E info@indewaag.nl
www.indewaag.nl
Daily from 10.00–01.00
10
Soups, salads, rolls (lunch); European full meals (dinner)
M Nieuwmarkt

Built in 1488, this magnificent multi-turreted edifice began life as St Anthoniespoort, one of three city gates. Closed every evening to keep out bandits and diseased riff-raff, it became redundant when the city walls were torn down and in 1617 became the new market square's weigh house. Its large terrace overlooks a farmers' market on Saturdays.

One room housed the city's militia, while others were given over to various guilds. The surgeons' hall, bearing the inscription *theatrum anatomicum*, is where Rembrandt painted his masterpiece, *The Anatomy Lesson of Dr Nicolaes Tulp* (1632), which hangs in the Mauritshuis in The Hague.

Three hundred candles, replaced twice daily, hang from the ceiling on improbably huge circular candelabras highlighting the grandeur. Long dining tables at the back enhance the ancient feel.

Lunch is basic but evening food is upmarket, focussing on steaks and fish. Opening hours may shorten if the diners have finished. We have been evicted by 23.00. It takes time to blow out all those candles.

All this history and grand architecture deserve a great beer and they don't come much finer than the golden-yellow **Westmalle Trappist Tripel** (9.5%), one of the earliest (some say *the* earliest) and best (some say *the* best) example of a blond tripel. Drier and more complex than most of its rivals it is made at the monastery of the same name in northern Antwerp.

75 Café Welling

J W Brouwerstraat 32

T 020 662 0155

www.cafewelling.nl

🕐 Sa–Su from 15.00; others from 16.00

🍷 15

🍴 Bar snacks

🚊 3, 5, 12, 16, 24 (Museumplein)

This quiet community pub is on a residential street behind the *Concertgebouw*, close to Museumplein. Inside, a large round table sits on the only carpet, in the middle of the wooden-floored bar, almost permanently occupied by a group of older regulars, usually engaged in deep philosophical discussions.

Portraits and paintings adorn the wood-panelled walls. Other furnishings consist of a mishmash of wooden tables and chairs, no two of which are alike, with light fittings just as jumbled. This is an interior assembled from a junk shop, which adds greatly to its appeal. There is no music either, making it even better.

Beware of Poes, the pub's unpredictable black cat, who may bound over and let you stroke him twice before taking your hand off with his teeth and claws. We bear the scars. The tropical fish in the tank behind the bar carry on oblivious to the carnage.

The beer list is limited in number because the barman only stocks what he likes. His tastes run to several 't IJ beers, Van Vollenhoven Extra Stout and all three beer from the Trappist abbey of St Rémy, near Rochefort. While the two stronger, more complex beers are fairly widespread, ■ **Rochefort 6** (7.5%), a dry, dark chocolate-brown brew is fairly rare, hinting at greatness and without knocking you for six. You should even survive more than one.

Café De Westerdok
Westerdoksdijk 715/A
T 020 428 9670
E cafe-westerdok@xs4all.nl
www.westerdok.eu
Fr–Sa 16.00–01.00; others 16.00–00.00
70+
None
48 (Barentszplein)

The Westerdok, a 10-minute walk or 3-minute ride west of Centraal station, deserves greater recognition as a beer hero. A convivial bar with a handful of tables, its counter is striking, five of its nine taps dispensing beers through founts shaped like ship's throttles. Full ahead/half astern kind of thing.

To the rear is mock Tudor, timbers interspersed with 80s-style panels. The ceiling fans are largely redundant now that smoking is only allowed in the basement billiard room. The painted scenes on the illuminated windows are a nice touch. A 50s radiogram sits on an occasionally active upright piano. A stuffed turtle is pinned to the wall. A stag's head still sports full Christmas regalia at Easter.

The changing beer selection is always good because enthusiastic, craft-beer-loving landlord Steve only stocks what he likes and, unusually for Amsterdam, is free to stock whatever he wants. The blackboard gives an idea of what is available but is updated slowly, so ask what's new.

The permanent choices include most Trappists, the Deliriums and several from St Bernard. Most Dutch cafés stock a fresh bock beer each autumn but here you may find a matured one too – a good idea. Our choice is a Belgian great, ■■ **Moinette Blond** (8.5%) from the excellent Dupont brewery near Tournai, arguably their finest beer. Beautifully rounded, it shows off the thumbprint yeast that sets it above most other strong blondes.

⑦ In De Wildeman ⑨
Kolksteeg 3
T 020 638 2348
E info@indewildeman.nl
www.indewildeman.nl
⊗ Closed Sunday
🕐 Fr–Sa 12.00–02.00; Mo–Th 12.00–01.00
🍷 218
🍴 Better light snacks
🚉 Amsterdam CS

The 'Wild Man' is one of the world's great beer bars and you should not leave Amsterdam without visiting it.

The smaller, cosier room is usually quieter. The larger has a tiled floor, gas lamp fittings and at the rear a raised area with a pile of old spirits casks. The absence of bar stools means that propping up the counter must be done standing, tasting room style.

The old beer bottles behind the bar feature now familiar brands from the days when they were ground-breaking. This was one of the bars that spearheaded the beer revolution. There are magnums, huge glasses too and a shelf of beer books.

Snacks include liver sausage, stuffed vine leaves, quiche, Stilton and *kabbanossi* – a kind of salami. On Saturdays a fishmonger may stop by.

The list of around 200 bottles and 18 taps, is roughly 60% Belgian, 25% Dutch and 15% other, changing steadily to ensure there are always discoveries to be made. Strong on smoked beers and other German oddities, it also has a good choice of gueuze.

Frank Boon rates his ▮▮ **Boon Oude Geuze Mariage Parfait** (8%) the best of his creations and we will not disagree. It represents the 'perfect marriage' of lambics from his finest casks to create a sparkling, refreshing, light amber drink with a citrus tang and the faintest resemblance to mainstream beer.

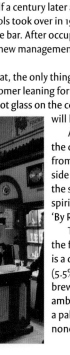

78 Wijnand Fockink
Pijlsteeg 31 & 43
T 020 639 2695
E contact@wynand-fockink.nl
www.wynand-fockink.nl

Tasting room: Daily 15.00–21.00.
Shop/distillery: Mo–Fr 10.00–17.00; Sa 13.00–18.00

3

Cheese, tapas

1, 2, 5, 9, 13, 14, 16, 17, 24, 25 (Dam Square)

Amsterdam's best tasting room is a tiny bar with sand on the floor and no seats, down an alley behind Dam Square's Krasnapolsky Hotel. Yes it is pronounced a bit like you think but ignore that. This is a supreme one-act play in wood and elegance.

The distillery that opened here in 1679 was taken over by Mr Fockink half a century later and became one of the greats. Sadly, when Bols took over in 1954 they dismantled it and in 1988 closed the bar. After occupation by squatters it re-opened in 1993 under new management, who added a new distillery and museum.

Besides chat, the only thing breaking the silence is the slurp of a customer leaning forward to take their first sip from the overfull shot glass on the counter. Don't gulp or your day will be over.

A copper vat washes glasses on the counter. Beers are dispensed from taps in the marble wall of a side room. The shelves bow under the stacked weight of the fifty or so spirits and liqueurs, many made 'By Royal Appointment'.

The beer options are counted on the fingers of one hand, though one is a diamond. ▮▮ **Special De Ryck** (5.5%), from the De Ryck family's brewery in East Flanders, is a light-amber brew of delicate bitterness – a pale ale without gimmickry that is nonetheless highly enjoyable.

79 De Zotte
Raamstraat 29
T 020 626 8694
www.dezotte.nl
Fr–Sa 16.00–03.00; others 16.00–01.00
130
Single plate meals (18.00–21.30)
1, 2, 5 (Leidseplein)

The 'Fool' is another of the city's top beer bars. A short hop from the bright lights of Leidseplein, here it is mainly candles that keep the place out of total darkness. The plasticated beer menus on the tables forego much of the need to read the menu on the far wall fortunately.

Barrels are stacked at the back and there are enamel signs everywhere. Those who enjoy the musical journey from Led Zeppelin to Nirvana via The Cure will be at home here. If that leaves you cold and you have no idea what RATM stands for, the beer list may soothe you to cheerful toleration of what is to some an infernal racket.

Food appears in the evening and may include homemade quiche, pasta, one meat dish and one fish.

The Flemish flag leaves you in no doubt where the

beer menu's heart lies, though some beers from Belgium's French-speaking south are there too. There are options from St Feuillien, Slaghmuylder, Halve Maan, Het Anker and several of the Trappist producers.

■■ Watou Kapittel Prior (9%) is a bit of a gem. A richly satisfying dark brown abbey beer from Van Eecke of West Flanders, it is sophisticated enough easily to hold its own alongside the most esteemed Trappists.

⑧⓪ Café De Zwart

Spuistraat 334

T 020 624 6511

🍷 Fr 09.00–02.00; Su 11.00–21.00; others 09.00–01.00

🍸 8

🍴 Apple pie, toasted sandwiches, bar snacks

🚋 1, 2, 5 (Spui)

'The Black' opened in 1921 and despite its name is not that dark at all. Rather, it is named after the family who originally owned it. This one-room corner café has Art Deco lighting, a vase of fresh tulips on the counter, a colourful mosaic floor and a curious semi-erotic oil painting.

The place is popular at night with a largely local crowd. By day it is a great place to sit quietly and read the paper, with a slice of apple pie. Emphasising the local feel, a message on the step in front of the bar counter reads: 'Nederland is moederland' – the Netherlands is the motherland.

Less presumptuous or grand than its neighbours, the Hoppe and the Luxembourg (above), its atmosphere is more like that of Antwerp's Oud Arsenaal, a place stuck in another time. There are enough brass coat hooks, occupying every available piece of wood-panelled wall space, to cater for the cloakroom needs of a visit from the Household Cavalry.

The only downside is the less-than-exciting beer list. While it will not win prizes without a bung, the draught version of ▮▮ **Tongerlo Dubbel** (6%), a dark brown top-fermented abbey beer from Belgium's largest independent brewery, Haacht, is dry and subtle enough to make an enjoyable session beer.

Featured breweries and beers

AMSTERDAM

de Bekeerde Suster
⑩ Manke Monnik (7.2%)

't IJ
(65) Columbus (9%)
⑤ Natte (6.5%)
㊹ Plzen (5%)
㊺ Struis (9%)
㊸ Zatte (8%)

de Prael
㊼ Abay Ethiopian Beer (6.6%)
㊿ Kop van Jut Blond (5.7%)
㉚ Mary (9.7%)
(60) Ooievaar Bier (7.5%)
(63) Willy (11%)

Snaterende Arend
⑧ Tempelbier (6%)

NETHERLANDS

Friese, *from Bolsward in Friesland*
② Us Heit Pels Speciaal (5.5%)

Gulpener, *from Gulpen in Limburg*
(70) Gerardus Wittems Kloosterbier Dubbel (7%)

Jopen, *from Haarlem*
㊾ Jopen Hoppen (6.8%)
(72) Jopen Koyt (8%)
⑱ Jopen Stout (5.5%)
(51) Jopen Winterbier (10%)

Klein Duimpje, *from Hillegom, near Haarlem*
⑯ Briljant Bier (7.2%)

Koningshoeven, *from Berkel-Enschot, near Tilburg in North Brabant*
(64) La Trappe Tripel (8%)

Lindeboom, *from Neer, in Limburg*
㊵ Venloosch Alt (4.5%)

de Molen, *from Bodegraven in South Holland*
㉒ Hel & Verdoemenis (10.2%)

de Schans, *from Uithoorn in North Holland*
(62) Van Vollenhoven Extra Stout (7%)

SNAB, *from Purmerend in North Holland*
⑥ Czaar Peter (9.5%)

Texelse Bierbrouwerij, *from the island of Texel in North Holland*
㊴ Texels Dubbel (6.4%)
(56) Texels Tripel (8.5%)

BELGIUM

Achel, *from Achel in Belgian Limburg*
㊱ Achel Blond (8%)

Achouffe (Duvel Moortgat), *from Achouffe in Belgian Luxembourg*
(67) La Chouffe (8%)
⑲ McChouffe (8.5%)

Affligem (Heineken), *from Affligem, west of Brussels*
(54) Affligem Christmas (9%)
(58) Affligem Dubbel (6.8%)

het Anker, *from Mechelen, south of Antwerp*
(59) Gouden Carolus Classic (8%)
(68) Gouden Carolus Tripel (9%)

du Bocq, *from Purnode in Namur*
⑨ Corsendonk Agnus (7.5%)

Boon, *from Lembeek, south of Brussels*
㊽ Boon Kriek (4.5%)
(77) Boon Oude Geuze Mariage Parfait (8%)
㉛ Boon Oude Lambiek (6%)

Bosteels, *from Buggenhout, NW of Brussels*
(52) Karmeliet Tripel (8.5%)
(55) Pauwel Kwak (8%)

Chimay, *from the Abbey of Scourmont in southern Hainaut*
① Chimay Bleue (9%)
⑮ Chimay Rouge (7%)

De Koninck (Duvel Moortgat), *from Antwerp*
(73) De Koninck (5%)

De Ryck, *from Herzele, near Ghent*
㊉ Special de Ryck (5.5%)

de Dolle Brouwers, *from Esen in West Flanders*
㉟ Oerbier (9%)

Drie Fonteinen, *from Beersel, south of Brussels*
⑳ 3 Fonteinen Oude Geuze (6%)

Dupont, *from Tourpes in western Hainaut*
㉚ Moinette Blond (8.5%)
㉞ Saison Dupont (6.5%)

Duvel Moortgat, *from Breendonk, west of Antwerp*
④ Duvel (8.5%)
㉑ Maredsous 8 (8%)
㉕ Maredsous 10 (10%)

Haacht, *from Boortmeerbeek NE of Brussels*
㉘ Tongerlo Dubbel (6%)

Halve Maan, *from Bruges*
㉛ Brugse Zot Blond (6%)
㉝ Straffe Hendrik (9%)

Huyghe, *from Melle, east of Ghent*
⑦ Delirium Tremens (9%)

Lefèbvre, *from Quenast in Wallonian Brabant*
㊻ Blanche De Bruxelles (4.5%)

Orval, *from the Abbey of Orval in Belgian Luxembourg*
㉛ Orval (6.2%)

Palm, *from Steenhuffel, NW of Brussels*
⑫ Palm Speciale (5.2%)

de Ranke, *from Dottignies, south of Kortrijk*
㉜ Guldenberg (8.5%)
㉙ XX Bitter (6.2%)

Rochefort, *from the Abbey of St Rémy at Rochefort in Namur*
㊆ Rochefort 6 (7.5%)
㊉ Rochefort 8 (9.2%)
⑪ Rochefort 10 (11.2%)

Rulles, *from Rulles in Belgian Luxembourg*
⑬ Rulles Estivale (5.2%)

Sint Bernard, *from Watou in West Flanders*
㉗ St Bernardus Abt 12 (10%)
㉔ St Bernardus Prior (8%)

Slaghmuylder, *from Ninove, west of Brussels*
㊳ Witkap Pater Dubbel (7%)
㊅ Witkap Pater Stimulo (6%)

Van Eecke, *from Watou in West Flanders*
⑰ Poperings Hommelbier (7.5%)
㊆ Watou Kapittel Prior (9%)
㊶ Watou's Witbier (5%)

Van Honsebrouck, *from Ingelmunster, north of Kortrijk*
❸ Kasteelbier Bruin (11%)

Van Steenberge, *from Ertvelde, north of Ghent*
㊷ Hesp Blond (7.9%)

Verhaeghe, *from Vichte, east of Kortrijk*
㊾ Duchesse de Bourgogne (6.2%)

Westmalle, *from the Abbey of Westmalle, NE of Antwerp*
㉖ Westmalle Trappist Dubbel (7%)
㊹ Westmalle Trappist Tripel (9.5%)

FRANCE

St Sylvestre, *from St-Sylvestre-Cappel, NW of Lille*
㊉ Trois Monts (8.5%)

GERMANY

Heller-Bräu Trum, *from Bamberg in Franconia*
㊅ Aecht Schlenkerla Rauchbier (5.1%)

König Ludwig, *from Fürstenfeldbruck in Bavaria*
㉓ König Ludwig Weissbier (5.5%)

Paulaner, *from Munich*
㉘ Paulaner Hefeweizen (5.5%)

USA

Flying Dog, *from Frederick in Maryland*
⑭ Doggie Style Classic Pale Ale (5.5%)

A stiff one to end with

Drinking in Amsterdam is not all about beer. There is a thriving tradition of spirits drinking too. The most famous creation was *jenever*, from which English gin is descended. It is named after the juniper berries used to flavour it and has nothing to do with that city in Switzerland.

Italian monks have been flavouring alcohol with juniper for a thousand years, but the idea was brought to the Low Countries by Dutch physician and alchemist Franciscus Sylvius (Sylvius de Bouve) in the 16th century. He distilled the alcohol content of the local hard liquor and added berries to create something palatable. First sold as a medicine it was another century before it was sold for its taste.

By the mid-1600s there were 400 distillers in Amsterdam. One of these, Lucas Bols, set up shop in a harbourside location outside the city in 1575. When exotic spices and fruits began arriving from the colonies, he used these to produce a huge variety of flavours, establishing a market lead the company never relinquished (although Remy Cointreau now run the show).

There remain around 60 smaller distillers in the Netherlands, all worth sampling. *Jenever* makers also produce no end of other spirituous liqueurs with fruit and herb flavours, from the sublime to the ridiculous.

The two basic types of *jenever* – *oude* (old) and *jonge* (young) – are distinguished not by age but the process used to make them. *Oude jenever* tends to have more character, while its *jonge* counterpart reflects the 20th century trend towards neutral, tasteless spirits, containing more unmalted grain and sugar and less malted barley in the distillate than *oude* versions.

Jonge jenever is usually served from a bottle kept in the freezer, often in a similarly chilled glass. A good *oude jenever* on the other hand can have as much complexity as a single malt Scotch, and is best served at room temperature.

Order a spirit or liqueur in a *proeflokaal* (tasting room) and it will be poured on the counter into a shot glass, almost to overflowing. There is no way you can pick this up without spilling it and you are not meant to try. Tradition demands you lean down and take the first sip by slurping from the glass (*nippen* or *slurpen*) without touching it with either hand. Once this is done, you may lift it to continue.

If you order a shot as a beer chaser, this is a *kopstoot* (a head butt). Do this too often and you will come to realise why.

Jenever is also where we get the term 'Dutch courage' from, originating among English troops who drank it while fighting alongside Dutch troops, to secure the protestant Netherlands' independence from Catholic Spain in the Eighty Years War.

Train
Station
500 m

Nassaulaan

Zoetestraat

Nieuwe Groenmarkt

Kruisstraat

Smedestraat

Jansstraat

⑰

㊝

Raaks

Jacobijnestraat

⑦①
⑱
Grote Markt
㉒

Grote of
Sint-Bavokerk

㊾

Gedempte Oude Gracht

Koningstraat

Barrevoetestraat

㊿
Botermarkt

Gedempte Oude Gracht

Lange Annastraat

Klein Heiligland

Groot Heiligland

⑯

Doelstraat

0   100 m

No. 81 in a series of 80

… Jopen's coming home

We had to omit one promising establishment for the simple reason that it was not built at the time of writing.

Within these pages you will find several references to Jopen being Haarlem's own brewery. But while their offices and spirit are there, they do not as yet have a brewhouse in the city. For now their beers are not actually brewed in the Netherlands, but by Van Steenberge in Belgium.

All is set to change, with spectacular plans to redevelop

a derelict church on the west side of Haarlem. The idea is to create a brewery with and an architecturally striking tap house. It is set to open by 2011 – check progress on

www.jopen.nl. If the artist's impressions are a true taste of what is to come, it will be well worth the wait.

Central Amsterdam

See next spread for inset of city centre

Quick tips for getting around

Most of our entries in the centre are within easy walking distance of one another and anyone able-bodied is likely to find their feet are the best way to get around. We also list the nearest bus and tram stops and tell you which lines stop there.

The only unusual service is the Stop/Go minibus that runs the entire length of Prinsengracht several times an hour in each direction. This has no regular stops – just flag it down anywhere you see it and once on board ask the driver to stop wherever you need get off.

Tickets bought on board (2010: €1,00) and are valid for one hour. The cheaper option is an OV-Chipkaart (www.ov-chipkaart.nl), similar to London Transport's Oyster Card, which you swipe each time you board and leave any bus or tram. Buy them pre-loaded at Centraal Station or at some magazine kiosks.

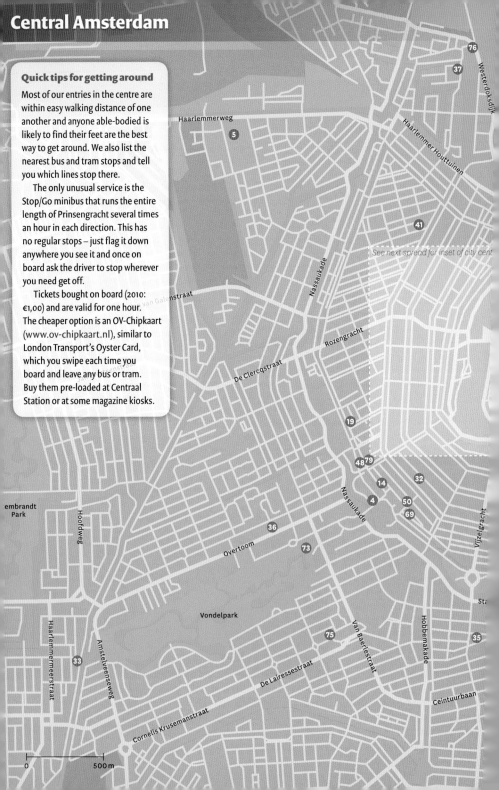

Westerdoksdijk

76

37

Haarlemmer Houttuinen

Haarlemmerweg

5

41

Nassaukade

Rozengracht

Van Galenstraat

De Clercqstraat

19

48 79

32

14

Nassaukade

4

50

69

Vijzelgracht

embrandt Park

Hoofdweg

36

Overtoom

73

Sta

Vondelpark

75

Van Baerlestraat

Hobbemakade

35

Haarlemmermeerstraat

Amstelveenseweg

33

De Lairessestraat

Ceintuurbaan

Cornelis Krusemanstraat

0   500 m

City centre Amsterdam

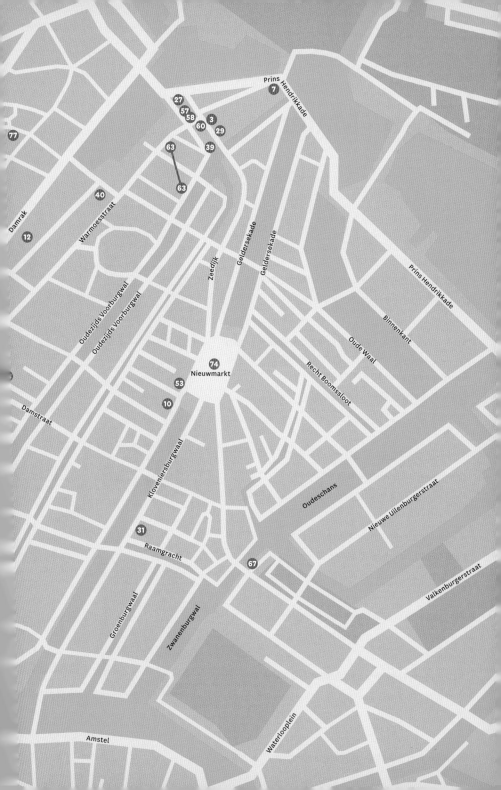

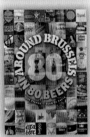